HANDBOOK TO SINGAPORE

HANDBOOK TO SINGAPORE

G. M. REITH
REVISED BY
WALTER MAKEPEACE

WITH AN INTRODUCTION BY
PAUL KRATOSKA

SINGAPORE OXFORD NEW YORK
OXFORD UNIVERSITY PRESS

Oxford University Press

Oxford New York Toronto
Petaling Jaya Singapore Hong Kong Tokyo
Delhi Bombay Calcutta Madras Karachi
Nairobi Dar es Salaam Cape Town
Melbourne Auckland

and associates in
Beirut Berlin Ibadan Nicosia

Originally published by Fraser and Neave, Limited, Singapore, 1892
Second edition 1907

First issued in Oxford in Asia Paperbacks *1985*
Reissued as an Oxford University Press paperback 1986
Second impression 1987

ISBN 0 19 582624 8

Printed in Malaysia by Peter Chong Printers Sdn. Bhd.
Published by Oxford University Press Pte. Ltd.
Unit 221, Ubi Avenue 4, Singapore 1440

INTRODUCTION

THE Reverend G.M. Reith's *Handbook to Singapore* was first published in 1892, and a new edition prepared by Walter Makepeace followed fifteen years later. Revisions to the original text were needed because Singapore was changing: 'the industries of the place have greatly developed; its old time buildings, and residential bungalows are rapidly disappearing, giving place to rows of buildings more suitable for housing the denser population', and 'the visitor has to go further afield to see native suburban life'. Makepeace wrote that 'the era of offices in flats and framework buildings' had set in, and it seems appropriate that this book should again be reissued at a time when those 'flats and framework buildings', no longer the symbol of a dynamic future but of a quieter and gentler past, are being replaced by high-rise towers created to accommodate a yet larger population and still expanding commercial enterprises.

Reith's book opens with a detailed account of the history and the administration of Singapore, much of it culled from Buckley's *Anecdotal History*[1] and contains lucid essays on Singapore's fauna (by William Davison, Curator of the Raffles Library and Museum) and flora (by the indefatigable H.N. Ridley, Director of Gardens and Forests), as well as a brief note on the geology of the island ('very disappointing to the student'). There is also a competent summary of the then current views on the Malay language.

Something of the character of the late Victorian traveller can be seen from the information Reith provides and the sights he

---

[1] Charles Burton Buckley, *An Anecdotal History of Old Times in Singapore 1819–1867*, reprint, Singapore, Oxford University Press, 1984.

recommends. The attraction was not Asia but European activities and accomplishments in Asia, and the city's main points of interest were the fruit of the Public Works Department's art. Reith directed his readers to government buildings, docks, roads and reservoirs, and ensured that they were amply supplied with facts about these edifices: the East Wharf was 500 feet in length with a depth at low water of 25 feet outside and 16 feet inside, the pumping station was 60 feet below the High Level Reservoir, the highest point on the island (Bukit Timah) had an elevation of 519 feet, and so on. For social life the visitor might choose from among the city's extraordinary range of clubs and societies: 'Very few places have so many Social Clubs and Institutions as Singapore compared with its European population'. The contrast between Reith's audience and a later generation of European visitor to Asia, doing the rounds of temple and bazaar, attending cultural shows, and relatively disinterested in public buildings or the local polity, could not be more marked.

The information supplied by Reith, abundant though it is, gives a curiously truncated view of Singapore. In his account of the workings of government, for example, he neglects to explain that one of the main sources of state revenue was the sale of licences for prostitution, gambling, opium and liquor, although he does mention that an arrangement of this sort was introduced in 1820. The commerce of Singapore, too, is no more than a shadowy presence, with far more said about failed proposals to tax trade than what was bought and sold, or by whom and to whom.

Reith's most egregious omission, however, is Singapore's non-European population, which is to say the great majority of the people resident in the city. They appear mainly as purveyors of curios, speakers of diverse languages, habitués of the native bazaars, and donors of civic amenities, a colourful but largely unremarked backdrop to the activities of Europeans. In 1901, however, the population of Singapore was slightly under 230,000, with Europeans accounting for less than 2 per cent of this total and the Chinese for 72 per cent. Singapore was in many respects a Chinese city with a European administration perched on its back like a mahout on the back of an elephant, firmly in control so long as its demands were reasonably in accord with what its charge was willing to do anyway.

A Chinese or Indian guidebook to Singapore at the turn of the century, if one existed, would show a substantially different city from that appearing in Reith's pages, and there are, in fact, two publications that can serve as a guide, or at least a gazetteer, to Singapore as it looked to its Asian residents during this period.[2] The inhabitants of Singapore, Europeans excepted, made minimal use of the names assigned to streets and buildings by the government, eschewing even such ethnically oriented names such as Cheah Hong Lim Street and Jalan Sultan, and in 1891 a list of 'native names' of roads and streets in Singapore was issued, followed in 1905 by a much fuller list of Chinese street and place-names. These terms, unlike most of the Malay words supplied by Reith, are neither translations nor renderings of English words but a set of expressions based for the most part on the characteristics of a locality, the principle work done there, for example, or its notable buildings.

The Chinese were blunter and less prudish than Reith, and the list of Chinese names shows features of Singapore life that he glossed over. To the Chinese the Police Office was the 'Chief Big Dog's Office' (lower-ranking policemen being simply 'dogs'), the Court of Requests was the 'Sue for Money Court' and the jail was the 'ankle-fetters building'. The Chinese Protectorate, dismissed by Reith as a 'plain and unpretentious' structure, was variously the office of the *Tai Jin* (Great Man), Pek-ki-lin (a Sinicized version of Pickering, the name of the first holder of the office of Protector of Chinese), or the Licence Office (because it was here that brothel licences were issued).

The roads of Singapore included 'Grinding Oil of Sesamum

---

[2] H.T. Haughton, 'Native Names of Streets in Singapore', *Journal of the Straits Branch of the Royal Asiatic Society*, No. 23, June 1891, pp. 49–65; H.W. Firmstone, 'Chinese Names of Streets and Places in Singapore and the Malay Peninsula', *Journal of the Straits Branch of the Royal Asiatic Society*, No. 42, February 1905, pp. 53–208.

Street' (Albert Street), 'the End of the non-Chinese Brothels' (Banda Street), 'Stone-Breaking Street' (Havelock Road), 'Scavenging Street' (Prinsep Street), 'Opium Kongsi' (Cecil Road, headquarters for the opium revenue farm), 'Slaughter Pig Depot' (Jalan Besar, near the Abattoir), 'Paint Wood Street' (a portion of South Bridge Road), and so on. Stamford Road was 'Flowing Water Street', a snide courtesy because water in the Stamford Road ditch normally did not flow.

Several streets were known by the temples and *kongsi* or society headquarters located there. Amoy Street was 'the Street behind the Temple of Ma-cho and Kun Yam', China Street—normally 'Gambling Hall Street'—was sometimes still called after the house of the defunct Ghee Hin Kongsi, while Clarke Street took its name from the Ghee Hok Kongsi, Upper Cross Street from the Hai San Kongsi, and Lavender Street (the 'Big Kongsi House in Rochore') from the Thien Ti Hui or Heaven and Earth League Hall.

Finally, the Chinese names for a few streets were picturesque almost to the point of being poetic: 'the Heavenly Place of the Five Generations' (Church Street), 'Golden Lily Temple' (Narcissus Street), 'Water-fairy Gate' (North Bridge Road), and 'Dragon's Head Fountain' (River Valley Road).

To its Tamil population Singapore's human topography was again different. Albert Street was 'the Place Where People Walk on Fire' (because of an annual fire-walking ceremony held there), Havelock Road was 'the Arrack (grain alcohol) Distilling Street', South Bridge Road 'the Cawker's Shop Street', Cross Street 'the Street of the Milk Shops', and Lavender Street 'the Potter's Street'. There was also a 'Street of the Flower Shops' (Arab Street), 'the Water Kampong' (Balestier Road), 'the Street of the Kampong Glam Old Hindu Theatre' (Rochore Road), 'the Street of the Dhobies' (launderers) (Queen Street), and 'the Street of the Temple of Krishna' (Waterloo Street).

Much has changed in Singapore since the publication of Reith's book, but the lineaments of the old city are still visible. The esplanade remains short-cropped and undisturbed, a playing field on what has become extremely valuable real estate. The Supreme Court and Municipal Office buildings now occupy the site of the old Hôtel de l'Europe alongside the esplanade, but St. Andrew's Cathedral has survived from Reith's day and at the far end of Orchard and Tanglin Roads the Botanical Gardens continues to provide an escape from the city which is not only refreshing but, in characteristic Victorian fashion, also instructive. Orchard Road itself is much changed. Where Reith found a 'long vista of high trees with their variegated foliage and cool shade' there is now a long vista of towering luxury hotels and shopping complexes. Elsewhere Singapore still glories in lush vegetation, but few visitors seeing its busy roads today are likely to be reminded of the 'quiet but effective' beauty of Devonshire lanes or the 'well-shaded avenue to an English mansion'.

As for Reith himself, very little information has come to light. He served as Pastor of the Presbyterian Church in Singapore from 1889 until 1896. In 1897 he published a book entitled *A Padre in Partibus*, a collection of articles written for the *Singapore Free Press* concerning a holiday in Java, Bali and the Celebes wherein he shows a nice wit and mines a seemingly endless stock of Scottish anecdotes and apophthegms. Reith was a founding member and the first secretary–treasurer of the Straits Philosophical Society, established on 5 March 1893, and a regular contributor to the *Free Press.*[3]

Reith's *Handbook to Singapore* is very much a product of its time, and so are its shortcomings. It concerns a small segment of Singapore, but that segment, which played a significant role in shaping the administration and society of the modern city, is now gone and firsthand accounts of its thinking and its interests are valuable. The disregard toward the Asian population is characteristic, and if Reith is unforthcoming about non-European life he is at least for the most part neutral, largely avoiding the sort of racial generalizations that were one of the least attractive features

---

[3] Walter Makepeace, R. St John Braddell and G.S. Brooke (eds.), *One Hundred Years of Singapore*, London, Murray, 1921, vol. 2, pp. 262, 287 and 301.

of the colonial period. In other respects he provides a competent guide to a colonial city and a colonial way of life of which there are many survivals, sometimes charming and sometimes disconcerting. Clubs, for example, remain a fixture in modern Singapore, and the older ones are fierce guardians of tradition. The virtues of Reith's book, then, are its evocation of this fading past, and as with most period pieces it is best to enjoy the book's virtues and disregard its failings.

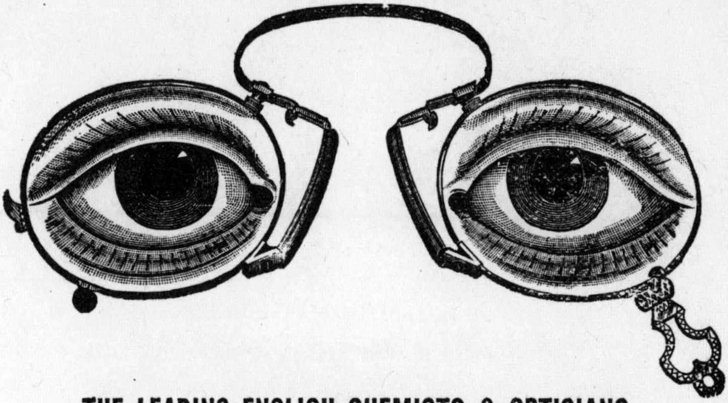

HANDBOOK

TO

SINGAPORE

WITH MAP

BY

THE REV. G. M. REITH, M. A.

SECOND EDITION

Revised by WALTER MAKEPEACE.

SINGAPORE.
FRASER AND NEAVE, LIMITED.
1907.

CONTENTS.

CHAPTER VI.

CHAPTER VII.

CHAPTER VIII.

CHAPTER IX.

CHAPTER X.

CHAPTER XI.

CHAPTER XII.

CHAPTER XIII.

CHAPTER XIV.

CHAPTER XV.

CHAPTER XVI.

MAP.

ILLUSTRATIONS.

PREFACE TO FIRST EDITION.

THIS handbook has been compiled specially for the benefit of visitors to Singapore, who have a few hours to a few days to spend in the town. It is intended to supply a felt want in Singapore; to give in a handy form some notes historical, descriptive, scientific, &c., in regard to the town and island; to afford what information is necessary to guide visitors during their stay, and to obviate some of the difficulties which travellers always encounter in a strange place. This work is the first of its kind published in the Settlement. The *Stranger's Guide to Singapore* by Mr. B. E. D'Aranjo (1890), and *Picturesque and Busy Singapore* by Mr. T. J. Keaughran, reprinted in 1887 from the *Straits Times*, are in circulation, but the former is more limited in its scope than the present work, and the latter too general to be of practical value as a guide-book. To both, however, this handbook is indebted for some of its information. The authority for the historical introduction is mainly a series of articles, entitled the *Anecdotal History of Singapore*, which appeared in the *Singapore Free Press* some years ago, from the pen of a well-known resident. The collection of reliable information has been a matter of some difficulty; but care has been taken to make the work as accurate as possible; and it is hoped that future editions, if they are called for, will correct the errors that may have crept into this edition, and render the work what it is intended to be, a useful *vade-mecum* for visitors to Singapore.

I am deeply indebted to W. Davison, Esq., of the Raffles Library and Museum, for his notes on the Singapore Fauna, an abridgement of which is in Chap. XIII.; and to H. N. Ridley, Esq., F.L.S., Government Director of Gardens and Forests, for his paper on the Flora and Geology of the island.

G. M. R.

SINGAPORE,

August, 1892.

PREFACE TO SECOND EDITION.

THE fifteen years that have passed since Mr. Reith's first edition of the Guide was issued have seen many changes in Singapore. The industries of the place have greatly developed; its old time buildings, and residential bungalows are rapidly disappearing, giving place to rows of buildings more suitable for housing the denser population that finds a livelihood in the place. The era of offices in flats and framework buildings has set in, and the visitor has to go further afield to see native suburban life. The shipping of the port has increased not merely in tonnage but in character, the modern replacing the old, iron ships wooden barks, and wire nails rotan pegs. The traveller will however find much to interest him in the native shipping that lies off Kampong Glam; and he who is bold enough to explore that neighbourhood, or indeed any part of the native town, with observant eye, will find in the manners and customs of the inhabitants a never-ending source of amusement and reflection in the humanity that swarms the streets of Singapore. The tropical vegetation, luxuriating within a stone's throw of the heart of the place can never cease to afford pleasure. The delightful suburban drives and walks, with their umbrageous beauty will continue to form the chief attraction of the place.

Since the issue of the first edition of this Handbook Mr. C. B. Buckley's *Anecdotal History of Singapore* has been issued in two large volumes. That will remain the permanent record of the place up to 1867. The reviser in common with every student of local history must needs express his indebtedness to Mr. Buckley's book on almost every point of the early life of Singapore.

W. M.

SINGAPORE,
June, 1907.

Photo by G. R. Lambert & Co.]

GOVERNMENT HOUSE.

Handbook to Singapore.

CHAPTER I.

Historical Introduction.

SINGAPORE* is an island lying off the southernmost extremity† of the Asiatic continent, from which it is separated by a narrow strait, varying in width from three quarters of a mile to two miles. It is one of the many islands that stud the sea between the Malay Peninsula and Australia. It is supposed, from the shallowness of the surrounding seas, and the nature of their flora and fauna, that Singapore, with the very much larger islands of Sumatra, Borneo and Java, not to mention the smaller islets that may be reckoned by the hundred around them, once formed part of the continent of Asia; while, for similar reasons, the Celebes, New Guinea, &c., were at one time united with Australia.

The island of Singapore lies about eighty miles north of the equator. It is oblong in shape, its greatest length (from east to west) being twenty-eight, and its greatest breadth (from north to south) fourteen miles.

*Singapore (Malay *Singapûra)* is said to mean "the City of Lions" (Sanscrit). There are no lions in the island, but as the natives use the word *Harimau* indiscriminately for "lion" and "tiger," it is possible that the word *Singha* or *Sinha* may have been as loosely used. But the derivation is not unchallenged.

† The southernmost point of the Malay Peninsula and of Asia is called *Tanjong Bulus:* it lies to the west of Singapore.

It occupies an unusually favoured position, being sheltered by Sumatra on the west from the storms that sweep over the Indian Ocean, and on the east by a spur of the Malay Peninsula from the typhoons that periodically disturb the China seas. Further, it is outside of the long volcanic belt that passes from Japan through the Philippines, and thence curves westward through Java and Sumatra.* Consequently the hurricane is unknown in Singapore, and earthquakes are of such rare occurrence—tremors occurred in 1862 and 1892—that residents are perhaps justified in continuing to assume that we are not in the belt of volcanic action.

The climate is moist; there is a heavy rain-fall extending over the whole year; and the temperature is moderate for a place in the heart of the tropics.

Singapore City is built on the south coast of the island, and faces the south-east. As the capital of the Straits Settlements,† it is the seat of the local government of the Colony and the residence of the High Commissioner for the Federated Malay States and Borneo.

Before the Settlement of the British in the Island, Singapore cannot be said to have had any history. It has a place in Malay legends,‡ according to which it

---

* The nearest point to Singapore of the volcanic belt is in the Karimon Islands, about 30 miles to the west, where there is a volcano which has long been quiescent.

† The Straits Settlements form a Crown Colony of the British Empire, and consist of the Dindings, Province Wellesley and Malacca in the Malay Peninsula, the islands of Penang (Prince of Wales' Island) and Singapore, with a few small islets in the Singapore Strait. Also, the Cocos or Keeling Islands and Christmas Island (added in 1886) in the Indian Ocean; and Labuan added in 1906.

‡ See the *Sejarat Malayu*, an English translation of which is to be found in Leyden's Malay Annals.

seems to have been a place of some note; it has the honour of mention in the great Portuguese Epic, the *Lusiad* of Camoens; but though a succession of Portuguese, Spanish, Dutch and British expeditions, both commercial and military, visited the Peninsula and the Archipelago from the beginning of the fifteenth to the beginning of the nineteenth century, the island of Singapore was passed by as if of little importance, until its occupation by the British in 1819.

The reference of Camoens to Singapore is in the tenth Canto of the *Lusiad*:—

> " But on her land's-end throned see Cingapur
> Where the wide sea-road shrinks to narrow way:
> Thence curves the coast to face the Cynosure*
> And lastly trends Aurora-ward its lay."
>
> (*Sir R. F. Burton's Translation.*]

" The island of Singapore is said to have been " settled about 1160 A.D. by Malays from Sumatra, Java, " or the neighbouring Johor Archipelago. The Settle- " ment was named Sinhapura (Lion City), and accord- " ing to old accounts, was large and prosperous. The " following century saw the conversion of the Malay " inhabitants of the Peninsula to Mahommedanism; " and in 1262, the colonists of Singapore were driven by " Javanese invaders to Malacca. At Malacca they " remained till the Portuguese conquest in 1511, when " they turned south again to what is now the territory " of Johor, and there founded a kingdom which included " their old home of Singapore."—Lucas: ***Historical Geography of the British Colonies.***

The British Empire owes the possession and the prosperity of Singapore to the foresight and energy of Sir Thomas Stamford Raffles. There is not space here

* The Cambodian Peninsula.

to give an account of his romantic and eventful career, only an outline can be given of his connection with the Settlement.* Raffles was sent to Penang as Assistant Secretary, by the East India Company, in 1805; in 1811, he was appointed Lieut-Governor of Java, and in 1817, having received the honour of knighthood, he was despatched to Bencoolen, a small British settlement on the south-west coast of Sumatra, as Lieut-Governor. While acting in this capacity, he was impressed with the necessity that the British should have a port in the Malay Archipelago to protect their trade, which was increasing yearly, between the Far East (China and Japan) and Europe and India. Ships from Europe to the China seas, after rounding the Cape of Good Hope, crossed the Indian Ocean, and thence passed through the Strait of Sunda between Sumatra and Java; while ships from India held their course down the Straits of Malacca, and through the Strait between Johore and the island of Singapore. Raffles thought a position on the island of Bintang, or somewhere in the neighbourhood, should be secured; and in 1818, he went to India to lay his plans before Lord Hastings, the Governor-General. Hastings authorised him to select a spot suited to his purpose; and as Bintang was occupied by the Dutch, who had established the Port of Rhio there to command the Archipelago, he fixed on the island of Singapore, owing to the excellent anchorage there; and concluded a treaty with the Maharajah of Johore, to whom the island belonged, transferring part of it to the British Government. On February 6th, 1819, the British flag was hoisted on the island; the

* It is unfortunate that Lady Raffles' biography of her husband is now out of print.

anniversary of which event is still observed as a public holiday in Singapore. "Our object" wrote Sir Stamford Raffles at this time "is not terri-"tory but trade; a great commercial emporium and "*fulcrum*, whence we may extend our influence "politically, as circumstances may hereafter require. "By taking immediate possession, we put a negative "to the Dutch claim of exclusion, and, at the same "time, revive the drooping confidence of our allies "and friends. One free port in these seas must "eventually destroy the spell of Dutch monopoly." For the first four years Singapore was a dependency of the Bencoolen Government; in 1823 it was transferred to the East India Company. The price paid for the island was $60,000 down, and a life annuity to the Sultan of $24,000.

The part of the island originally ceded to the British was a strip of land about five miles in length, stretching along the sea-coast from Mount Palmer to Tanjong Katong. The opposition of the Dutch to the British Settlement on Singapore was so strong that the Home Government at first declined to sanction it; the Calcutta officials were hostile, and indeed the Settlement might have been broken up, had it not been for the dogged obstinacy of its founder, who persisted, on his own responsibility, in maintaining his position. In 1824, however, the Dutch and British Governments came to an agreement; the Malay Archipelago was divided between the rival powers, and though Holland secured the lion's share of territory, England remained in possession of the most important positions on the eastern route, and especially, Singapore. Sir Stamford Raffles died in England in 1826, at the comparatively early age of forty-five. The annals of British influence in the East contain the name of no man who in so short a life-time accomplished so much. The following pages will furnish many instances of his wisdom, philanthropy, and administrative genius.

The population of Singapore, when Sir Stamford Raffles hoisted the British flag in the island, was under 200. A Malay *kampong* or village at Teluk Blangah, where the P. & O. S. N. Co.'s wharf now is, seems to have been the only inhabited spot, for the island was wooded to the water's edge. At that time there were not fifty Chinamen in the place. It is hard to realize as we pass through the streets of the busy, populous city, that ninety years ago there was hardly one man to every two square miles on the island. Only a year after the landing of Sir Stamford Raffles the population had risen to 5,000.

The first of the now many European trading firms was founded by an enterprising Scotchman—Mr. A. L. Johnston—who established himself in the Settlement a few months after its acquisition. The firm A. L. Johnston & Co. survived to the year 1892.

From the beginning, Singapore has been a free port; no duties of any kind are levied. The policy of Sir Stamford Raffles in this respect finds its justification in a comparison of the progress and general importance of the Dutch and French with the British Settlements in the Far East. There have been several attempts to levy customs, but the good sense of the mercantile community has hitherto prevented the adoption of so suicidal a policy.*

---

* There is a small charge on all vessels entering the port for the up-keep of the Light-houses in the Straits; but payment is not grudged, for navigation in dangerous waters is made safe by the numerous lights that stud the channel.

The year 1820* saw the establishment of Gambling, Opium, and Spirit Farms, though somewhat against Sir Stamford Raffles' inclination, and in the same year another well-known European firm was founded by Mr. Alexander Guthrie, whose name survives in the present local style of the firm—Guthrie & Co., which was converted into a limited company, without any change of proprietorship, however, in 1902.

The progress of Singapore must have been very rapid in these early days, for we find the population estimated at 10,000 in 1822. From 200 to 10,000 in three years is a considerable advance.

The next year (1823) was important in many respects. A Chinaman, Seah Eu Chin, is said to have started gambier and pepper planting on the island, an industry which had much to do with the early prosperity of the Settlement.

The increasing population demanded some regular form for the administration of justice; and in this year five European magistrates were appointed, of whom two had to sit with the Resident (then Colonel Farquhar) in court. The composition of juries in those days was either five Europeans, or four Europeans and three respectable natives.

Sir Stamford Raffles had in his mind, from the beginning of the Settlement, a scheme for native education, which took practical shape shortly before his departure in the foundation of the Raffles' Institution. $17,500 were subscribed for this object, and grants of land to endow the school were given.

---

* An interesting though not wholly reliable history of the acquisition of Singapore, and the first few years of its occupation by the British was written by a Malay teacher named Abdullah. The *Hikayat Abdullah* (so the book is named) is ordinarily used as a reading book by students of Malay.

One of the last acts of Sir Stamford Raffles was the abolition of slavery. He left Singapore about the middle of the year, to the great regret of all who had known his just and kindly rule.

The island of Singapore was finally ceded to Britain, on August 3rd, 1823, and a grant of 56 acres, in Kampong Glam was assigned to the Sultan. An attempt of the Dutch to occupy Johore came to nothing.

In 1824 appeared the first issue of a local newspaper, *The Singapore Chronicle.* It was originally published fortnightly. This year witnessed the settlement of the rival claims of Dutch and English to various possessions in the Malay Archipelago by the Treaty of Holland. England ceded Sumatra to the Dutch, and all the islands south of the Singapore Strait ; while Holland relinquished her Indian possessions, gave up Malacca, withdrew her protest against the British occupation of Singapore, and ceased all political intercourse with the Peninsula. The treaty in later years was the cause of many diplomatic quarrels between England and Holland, without, however, producing any serious rupture.

In 1826, Penang, Malacca, and Singapore were united under one Government, with Penang as capital. The population of Singapore at this time was computed at 13,732.

The first Criminal Sessions, and the first infliction of the death penalty, occurred in 1828, when a Kling* and a Chinaman were hanged for murder. At this

* The name *Kling* is given in Malay to immigrants from the Coromandel coast. It is derived from the old emigration port Kalingapatam.

period, and for many years later, the neighbouring seas were infested by pirates. In their light *prahus* the Malay sea robbers swooped down upon passing ships, and then took refuge in the many creeks and inlets with which the Peninsula and the islands of the Archipelago abound. The Government sent expeditions against them, and private enterprise joined with the Government in waging a war of extermination against these highwaymen of the seas. Great credit is due to the Chinese merchants who about this time fitted out and manned a few junks to meet, and to pursue to their haunts, the piratical *prahus*. Against these junks the *prahus* were powerless, and the pirates lost much of their prestige.

Even now occasional piracies occur; but they are few and far between. The age of steam and the rapid increase of traffic on the Eastern seas give few facilities for piracy and ensure swift vengeance on the pirates.

Tigers, which were for a time the curse of Singapore, began to molest the inhabitants about the year 1831, by which time the population had increased to more than 20,000. The interior of the island was then as little known to the inhabitants as Central Africa was to Europeans a few years ago. It was covered with dense jungle; but, as the increase of population demanded a clearing of the jungle, these savage denizens of the forest began to give trouble. The tiger has been nearly exterminated by this time; but occasionally one is shot by local sportsmen, and more rarely, from time to time, news comes from the plantations of a coolie being carried off by a man-eater.

Tigers have been seen and shot in the Town itself, but they escaped from cages. Outside municipal limits, however, they are still sometimes found, and one or two local shikaries have the earliest *khabar* (news) brought to them of Stripes' tracks. The animal is not uncommon in Johore, and the Sultan of that State has a record of these fierce animals to his gun that will compare favourably with the record of many of the sport-loving potentates of India.

In 1832, Singapore, by reason of its rapid growth, was made the capital of the Straits Settlements, in place of Penang, which had held that honour for six years.

To meet pressing necessity a Court of Requests was established in the Settlement in 1834.

In the same year, the Bishop of Calcutta visited Singapore; and as a result of this visit, it was resolved to found a church. Previous to this time there had been a missionary in the Settlement, who acted as Colonial Chaplain, and conducted Divine Service in the Mission Chapel. The Bishop consecrated the old cemetery on Fort Canning, which had been in use since 1822, and which continued in use till 1867. The proposed church was founded in 1835, and consecrated by the Bishop of Calcutta, on a second visit, in 1838. The Armenian Church of St. Gregory, which still stands in Hill Street, was consecrated in 1836, services having been held since 1821.

The rapid development of trade at the port led to the formation of a Chamber of Commerce in 1837; and in the following year Mr. Waghorn's suggestion of the Overland Route between Europe and the East began to be seriously discussed. It is curious to read how the mercantile community in Singapore regarded this proposal, together with another, somewhat earlier, the use of steam-ships. Both of these, which have done so much for Singapore, were looked upon with suspicion and distrust, and were even regarded as foolish dreams. It is a strange commentary also on human gratitude that Mr. Waghorn was allowed to die in abject poverty, though many were enriched by his suggestion.

In 1840, the population was estimated at 39,681; at that time the chief European residences stood on Beach Road and in the neighbourhood of Kampong Glam. No attempt seems to have been made to penetrate north-wards into the island, until in 1843 a road to *Bukit Timah* (Hill of Tin), six miles inland, was opened for traffic. Horses were first imported into Singapore in 1844. In 1845, the Peninsular and Oriental Steam Navigation Company started a mail service to the Far East, the s.s. *Lady Mary Wood* arriving at Singapore in August of that year. This marks a new era in the commercial prosperity of the Settlement. In the same year the *Straits Times* newspaper, which still holds its place as one of the chief journals in the Straits, was founded as a weekly, the *Singapore Free Press* dating ten years previous to that.

The next year saw another event of commercial importance,—the establishment of the Oriental Bank in Singapore, which was a great convenience to local merchants and traders, there being hitherto no bank in the place. In 1847 two additions were made to the public buildings of the town—the Cathedral of the Good Shepherd (founded in 1843), and a Gaol at Sepoy Lines, which is now included in the area occupied by the present Criminal Prison.

Singapore was visited in 1850 by Lord Dalhousie, the Governor-General of India, in commemoration of whose visit an obelisk was built, which now stands near the Cricket Pavilion on the Esplanade. It is a landmark for ships anchoring in the Roads and when the Esplanade was widened by a reclamation in 1894, was removed a few yards from its original position, The foundation of the Horsburgh Light-house* was laid on the rock of *Pedra Branca*, which lies in mid-channel between Cape Romania and the island of Bintang. The light-house was named after the well-known hydrographer, James Horsburgh, F.R.S., by whose charts the dangers of the difficult navigation in the neighbouring seas were reduced to a minimum. The light was first put into use in October, 1851.

Chinese Secret Societies began to give trouble about this time. The successes of the Roman Catholic Missionaries† amongst the Chinese in the country districts caused a fanatical persecution of the converts, at the instigation of the Secret Societies. Conversion to Christianity removed the proselyte from the authority of these *Kong-sees* to the protection of the priests; and to prevent further conversions, the Chinese rose and plundered the property of their Christian countrymen, burning their houses and

* Horsburgh Lighthouse, white flash light (one flash in ten seconds). Lat. 1° 20″ N., Long. 104° 24′ 30″ E. Dioptric lens of first order. It is 36 miles East of Singapore town, and its height from high water to centre of light is 101 feet. The name of the rock on which it is built is a Portuguese translation of the Malay name *Batu Puteh*, *i.e.*, the White Rock.

† The Roman Catholic Missions were at this time, as they are still, the largest and most active in the Colony. In 1851, the Portuguese Church of St. Joseph was founded, and placed under the jurisdiction of the Bishop of Macao. A new Church is in course of erection at the present time. The School of St. John was started in the same year by the French Mission.

plantations, stealing their goods and money, adding acts of violence and murder to their robberies. The insurgents came into collision with bodies of police and marines, and were ultimately reduced to order. Much of the stolen property was recovered and restored to the owners.

Three years later (1854) the most serious riot that has ever occurred in the history of the Colony, broke out through a trifling bazaar dispute between a Hokkien and a Macao.* The rapid increase of the Chinese population was fraught with considerable danger to the peace of the community, chiefly because of tribal feuds between the different clans, which often led to violence and blood-shed. The bazaar-dispute became the excuse for a war between the rival factions, and the fighting lasted for more than a week. The Governor—Colonel W. J. Butterworth, to whom the Settlement owed much of its early prosperity—did not believe the danger so great as it turned out to be, and delayed taking decisive steps to check the riot, with the result that the riot, which might have been suppressed in a few hours, lasted without intermission for eight days; and the suppression involved considerable loss of life on both sides. From the town the insurrection spread to the country districts; business was suspended; the offices shut and strongly guarded, the European residents were enrolled as special constables, Malays and Indians were armed, and for a few days the island was in a state of war. Many arrests were made; about 250 prisoners were brought to trial, but only two were executed, most

* That is a native of the province of Hok-kien, and a native of Quantung.

of the rest being sentenced to long terms of imprisonment with hard labour, and some transported.

The Verandah Riots* in 1888, show that the Chinese population, law-abiding as a rule, may at any moment be a serious trouble to the Settlement; they, too, were unnecessarily prolonged by the indecision of those responsible for the peace of the town.

In 1889, Sir Cecil Smith determined to legislate for societies of all kinds. The only associations that can legally be formed are (*a*) Registered Societies; with responsible head-men liable to be called on to render an account of their doings; (*b*) Societies exempted from Registration, mostly well-known clubs and social organisations. That illegal societies do still exist is shown by occasional prosecutions in the Police Courts. The Chinese habit of forming guilds or associations for mutual defence and attack extends to domestic servants and burglars and the Criminal Investigation Department has to be on the *qui vive* to check these illegal societies, who, however, possess nothing like the power or influence they did even ten years ago.

Soon after the riots of 1854, it was considered expedient to have a volunteer corps of European residents in Singapore; and a rifle corps was accordingly formed. In the same year, navigation in the Straits was rendered safer by the foundation of the Raffles' Light-house on a small rock in the Straits of Malacca, some twelve miles west of the town. It was much needed, for the sea in that region is full of small islands and shoals.

---

* So-called because the Municipality of Singapore insisted that the verandahs in the streets of the Chinese quarters should be cleared of the goods and stalls with which they are usually crowded, to make way for foot passengers. The riots lasted for three days.

The foundation-stone of the original Town Hall was also laid in this year, though the building was not completed till 1861.

An unsuccessful attempt was made by the Indian Council to substitute the rupee for the Mexican dollar which had been the local currency in the Archipelago long before there was a British Settlement. The proposed change was stoutly resisted by the Singapore merchants, and subsequently dropped. This attempt had much to do with a proposal mooted for the first time in the following year (1855) that the Straits Settlements should be transferred from the Indian Government to a government which should be directly responsible to the Crown. A public meeting was held in Singapore, and resolutions to that effect were carried by acclamation. The reason of the proposal is declared in the words of the resolutions:—"This "meeting is forced into the painful conviction that "the Legislative Council of India in treating with "utter disregard the remonstrances of the inhabi-"tants, have shown that they are neither to be "moved by any prospect of doing good, nor restrained "from doing evil to the Straits Settlements; and that "it is, therefore, the painful duty of this community "to use every exertion, and to resort to every means "within their reach to obtain relief from the mis-"chievous measures already enacted, and to escape "from the infliction of others of the same nature, "more comprehensive and still more hurtful."

The Indian Council again attempted to over-ride public opinion in Singapore, by the imposition of port-dues, a policy which was thought disastrous by the local traders, it being regarded as a *sine qua non* from the time of Sir Stamford Raffles downwards, that Singapore should be a free port. A spirited protest addressed to the Imperial Government led to the abandonment of the proposal.

The Straits Settlements were made a Crown Colony in 1867, and placed under the direct control of the Colonial Office; though by their constitution, the Settlements have scarcely any more voice in the management of their affairs than they had under the Indian Council: for the official members—a majority in the Legislative Council—are bound to vote as the Secretary for the Colonies *pro tem.* directs.

The old English Church in Singapore had become unfit for public worship by this time, the congregation being compelled to use the Court-house for Divine Service.* The Indian Council voted the sum of Rupees 47,000 for the erection of a new building. The remainder of the cost was defrayed by public subscription, and the foundation of St. Andrew's Cathedral was laid in the following year (1856). The building was opened for worship in 1862.

In 1858, the Patent Slip and Dock Company, subsequently known as the New Harbour Dock Co., was incorporated, and six years later, the Tanjong Pagar Dock Company, both of which have contributed

* A curious illustration of the superstitions prevalent amongst the uneducated Chinese may be quoted in this connection. It was widely believed that the English had deserted their Church through fear of the demons that haunted it; and that it was the purpose of the Government to sacrifice a number of human heads to propitiate the demons. A panic seized the populace: men were afraid to go out after dark lest they should fall victims to the English sacrifice. It was long before the Government and the educated Chinese succeeded in allaying the fears of the people. These panics periodically arise, the last being when the Singapore-Kranji railway bridges were being built, their foundation being said to require human heads to give the required stability.

largely to the commercial importance of the city, although they have not altogether kept pace with modern requirements. The two great Dock Companies were amalgamated and possessed a controlling influence over the Slipway Co., at Tanjong Rhu. In 1905 the Government expropriated the property of the Company, and took over its management. The Court of Arbitration, presided over by Sir Michael Hicks Beach, awarded the shareholders the sum of twenty-nine million dollars for their property, which is now managed by a Board consisting of the leading merchants and shippers, with some Government officials.

The Scotchmen in the town organised a Presbyterian congregation in the following year (1859), and worshipped for a time in the Old Residency Chapel in Bras Basah Road, the use of which was granted them by the Government at the hours when it was not used by the Anglican congregation. The present Presbyterian Church was built in 1878.

The transfer of the Colony from the Indian Government to the Crown was made in accordance with the report of Sir Hercules Robinson, then Governor of Ceylon, who was sent to the Straits to enquire into the state of affairs. The first Governor after the change was General Sir Harry Ord. It would appear from the local press of the time, that he carried matters with a high hand, and embroiled himself with the commercial community by the way in which he pressed forward his plans for administrative reform. The monument of his rule is Government House. In 1873, the system of administering justice in the Colony was revised; The High Sheriff, grand and petit juries gave way to the present system. (*See* Chapter II.) In the same year General Sir Andrew Clarke arrived in Singapore as Governor. His name will be associated with the development and prosperity of the Malay Peninsula, for he established what ultimately became the Residential system in the Malay States,* by means of which order and good government were introduced and the foundation of material prosperity laid. The result has justified Sir Andrew Clarke's policy. From 1874 to the present time the progress of the Native States has been remarkably rapid. The Residential system took definite shape after the Perak war which broke out in 1875, owing to the murder of Mr. J. W. W. Birch, the first British Resident in that country, and the disturbed condition of Sungei Ujong. The Governor at this time was Sir William Jervois, whose energetic administration bore good fruit in latter days; especially in the matter of Colonial defences. In 1877, occured a great fire at Tanjong Pagar Dock, which lasted for 28 days, baffling all endeavours to extinguish it. On April 13, a Chinese coolie smoking in one of the attap-roofed coal sheds, accidentally set fire to the building. The coal soon kindled, and till May 12 the fire continued, consuming during the time about 50,000 tons of coal with the sheds in which it was stored.

Sir William Jervois† was succeeded by Sir William Robinson, whose bad health compelled him

---

* The Protected Native States were Perak, Selangor and Sungei Ujong on the West Coast of the Peninsulā, Pahang on the East Coast and Negri Sembilan (including Jelebu, Rembau, Johol and Sri Menanti) to the East of Sungei Ujong and Selangor. These were finally Federated in 1897, Sir Frank A. Swettenham, subsequently Governor of the Straits Settlements, being the first Resident-General.

† Col. Anson, afterwards General Sir Arch. Anson, twice held office as Acting Governor, in 1877 and 1879 to 1880.

to leave the Colony in 1879, and Sir F. A. Weld was appointed in his place in 1885.

From 1879 to 1889, reclamation works were carried out on an extensive scale, first from Collyer Quay towards Tanjong Pagar by running a sea-wall across what used to be called Teluk Ayer and filling up the tidal swamps; and then by running another sea-wall from the north side of the Singapore river towards Beach Road, thereby reclaiming many acres of valuable land, and adding to the beauty of the Esplanade. During the same period some new public buildings were erected, and others added to and enlarged, to the great improvement of the general appearance of the city.

In 1893 there were two great fires, in Market Street and McAlister's in Battery Road, and in the following year St. Matthew's Church, Sepoy Lines, was consecrated. The rebellion in Pahang caused much excitement also in 1894, while the Colony was in the throes of a period of non-prosperity and a greatly enhanced military contribution, which led to the resignation of four Unofficial Members of Council and all the visiting justices. So late as 1896 a tiger was shot at Mount Pleasant, on the Thomson Road. In 1900 the first sod of the Singapore-Johore Railway was cut and the Municipality purchased the Gas Company's Works.

In February, 1888, the Verandah Riots, already referred to (p. 14), broke out; and in the same month the Singapore Volunteer Artillery Corps was enrolled.

The Corps has fairly well maintained its strength. Originally it formed part of the fixed defences and drilled with the old 7-inch muzzle loading gun, a weapon of that type being placed where the new Shipping Office now stands. The battery of four maxim guns were presented by the Sultan of Johore, and some generous Chinese. The corps is now attached to the mobile defence and mans a battery of 10 pr. breech-loading mountain guns. The original Singapore Volunteer Rifles was disbanded about this time.

In 1898 the Singapore Volunteer Rifles were formed, but ceased to exist in 1904. The Singapore Volunteer Corps now consists of the S. V. A., the S. V. A. Maxim Company, the Singapore Royal Engineers (Volunteers), the Singapore Volunteer Infantry (two companies, Eurasian and Chinese) and the Cadet Corps. There is also a company at Penang.

The Chinese Secret Societies' Ordinance was passed by the Legislative Council in 1889, and a proclamation ordering the disbanding of these troublesome organisations by January 1, 1890, was posted throughout the town in November. In the following year (March) T.R.H. the Duke and Duchess of Connaught, on their way home from India, visited Singapore. The Duke of Connaught inspected the fortifications of the town, and in commemoration of his visit the principal Fort on Pulau Blakang Mati was named after him. H. R. H. the Duke of York, in his tour through the Colonies, stayed at Singapore in 1901. Prince Arthur of Connaught, on a mission to Japan, called here in 1906.

The Singapore-Kranji Railway was completed and opened (Tank road to Woodlands, opposite Johore Bahru) in 1905. The extension to the Docks was completed in the following year.

Improvements in the town and neighbourhood are being carried on rapidly; but these are too numerous to be particularised here.

***

Between 1857 and 1860, the prosperity of Singapore sustained a severe check through the failure of the nutmeg crop. The trees were destroyed by a blight; and the cultivation of the nutmeg is now practically at an end in the Island. Pepper, gambier, indigo, spices, liberian coffee, tapioca, &c., with cocoanuts, pine-apples and other fruits are cultivated to some extent: the prosperity of Singapore does not, however, depend on these, but on the fact that it is the great *entrepôt* for Eastern commerce, and an important coaling station. Its position and harbour secure both its importance and its prosperity; and few of the outposts of the British Empire can show such a record of growth and progress as Singapore. Like the rest of the world, it has its ups and downs through the depression of trade, and the consequent diminution of its revenues; but to use a hackneyed expression commonly applied to the Colony, its prosperity progresses by leaps and bounds. The development of the Native States, and the further opening up of the Malay Peninsula, which contains great mineral wealth, has re-acted favourably upon Singapore; and it is not too much to hope that the future of the town will eclipse its past.

CHAPTER II.

The Government—The Garrison and Defences—Justice—The Municipality of Singapore—Police—Revenue.

FROM 1819 to 1867, the Straits Settlements were governed by the Indian Council; but in 1867, they were erected into a Crown Colony, the Local Government being vested in a Governor,* an executive of eight Members appointed by the Crown, assisted by a body of seven unofficial Members of Council (two of whom are elected by the Chambers of Commerce in Penang and Singapore for nomination, and the rest nominated by the Governor.)

---

* Previous to 1867, the Local Governors in the Colony were :—

Mr. Robert Fullerton ...	1826
Mr. S. Ibbetson	1828
Mr. K. Murchison	1833
Mr. Sam. G. Bonham ...	1837
Col. W. J. Butterworth ...	1843
Mr. E. A. Blundell	1855
Col. Cavenagh	1861

Since 1867, the following have held the Office :—

Gen. Sir Harry St. George Ord, G.C.M.G.	1867-73
Col. Sir Andrew Clarke, R.E., K.C.M.G., C.B. ...	1873-75
Gen. Sir Wm. F. D. Jervois, R.E., G.C.M.G.... ...	1875-77
Sir Wm. C. F. Robinson, K.C.M.G.	1877-79
Sir Fred. A. Weld, G.C.M.G.	1885-87
Sir Cecil Clementi Smith, G.C.M.G.	1887-93
Sir Charles Bullen Mitchell, G.C.M.G	1894-98
Sir Frank Athelstane Swettenham, K.C.M.G. ...	1901-03
Sir John Anderson, K.C.M.G....	1904

The Executive consists of:—

H. E.* the General Commanding the Troops;

The Hon. the Colonial Secretary;

Do. Resident Councillor of Penang;

Do. Resident Councillor of Malacca;

Do. Attorney-General;

Do. Colonial Treasurer;

Do. Auditor-General;

Do. Colonial Engineer and Surveyor-General;

These, with the seven unofficial Members of Council form the Legislative Body of the Colony.

The system of governing a Colony from Downing Street secures a permanent official majority in cases where there is a difference of opinion between the Colonial Office and the residents on important questions.

***

The Colony contributes to the Imperial Government 20 per cent. of its revenue as a Military Contribution, besides spending considerable sums locally for land and housing the troops. In 1905 this amounted to $1,923,994. In the same year the Volunteers cost $61,514. There are stationed at Singapore a European Battalion; an Indian Battalion; two companies of the Royal Garrison Artillery; a company of Royal Engineers; a company of Asiatic Artillery, with representatives of the various army departments, in all about 2,000 men.

The Infantry is quartered in the large barracks at Tanglin, and on the Alexandra Road. The artillery

* The G. O. C. is styled "His Excellency" in the Straits Settlements, as well as the Governor.

is stationed at Fort Canning and Blakang Mati; the Engineers on Pulau Brani, where the Ordnance Store is. The whole force is under the command of Major-General R. Inigo Jones, C.V.O., C.B.

The Town and harbour are defended by forts clustered round the wharves, docks, and coal-stores. In the heart of the town at a height of 156 ft. is Fort Canning, formerly called Government Hill, now used as a barracks for a part of the Garrison Artillery and as the general signal-station for the town. From this fort all salutes are fired and the noon time-gun (1 p.m. on Sundays). There is a light-house for vessels making the port and a flag-staff for signalling the arrival and departure of ships, &c. Fort Canning is, however, of no military value in the defences, now.

Between Johnston's Pier and Tanjong Pagar Dock is Fort Palmer, on a crag about 120 feet high, overhanging the sea and guarding the eastern entrance to New Harbour. To the west of the harbour is fort Pasir Panjang. The other forts stand on the islands of Blakang Mati and Pulau Brani.

A gun-boat or cruiser from the China Station usually lies in the Roads, and the harbour is well-protected by submarine mines and torpedoes. The main objection of the Calcutta authorities in 1819, to Sir Stamford Raffles' settlement in Singapore, was that the harbour could not be properly defended. The objection has been removed in recent years to a very considerable extent.

***

The law of the Colony is made or modified by Ordinances of the Legislative Council, subject to the approval of the Crown. Criminal cases are tried under the Indian Penal Code (slightly modified to meet local conditions); and the Civil Procedure Code of the Colony is based on the English Judicature Acts.

The Courts of Law in the Settlements are of six kinds:—The Supreme Court; Courts of Requests (for sums not exceeding $100); Courts of two Magistrates or Bench Courts; Coroners' Courts; Magistrates' Courts; and Justices of the Peace. The Supreme Court, consisting of a Chief Justice and three Puisne Judges, sits regularly in Singapore, where the Chief Justice and one of the Puisne Judges are usually in residence; holds assizes every two months; and when required acts as a Court of Appeal and a Vice-Admiralty Court.

***

The Municipal Commission of Singapore is partly an elective body, some Commissioners being elected by the rate-payers in the different wards, and others, with the President, appointed by H. E. the Governor. The water-supply of the town is under its control; also, the up-keep of roads and bridges within Municipal limits; the supply of gas and electricity. The Municipality has power to levy rates and taxes; and in addition to the water rate, its revenue comes from assessments on house property, market farms, a horse and carriage tax, registration of bullock-carts and all vehicles plying for hire, dog licenses, and licenses for offensive and dangerous trades. In 1905 the total revenue was $2,556,995, and the total expenditure $2,551,606, the indebtedness being $3,332,500.

The Municipal area is about 28 square miles; it extends $4\frac{1}{2}$ miles E., W. and N. of the Town Hall. It is divided into five wards:—

1. Tanjong Pagar.
2. Central Ward (includes the European business quarter and, roughly, that part of the town between Orchard Road and River Valley Road).
3. Tanglin (between Orchard Road and Bukit Timah Road).
4. Rochor, at the N. E. end of the town.
5. Kalang, beyond Rochor.

***

The Police Force of the Straits Settlements is made up of a small European contingent with over 2,000 Asiatics, consisting of Sikhs, Malays, Klings and a few Chinese. At the head is the Inspector-General under whom are a Chief Police Officer, 2 Superintendents, 4 Assistant Superintendents, 2 Chief Inspectors, and 10 Inspectors (all Europeans). Of the Asiatics, the Sikhs are generally considered the most efficient and reliable Police. In the Town and Island of Singapore there are 35 Police Stations; the Central Station being in South Bridge Road opposite the Magistrates' Courts.

***

The actual revenue for 1905 was $11,657,423 of which the principal items are opium and spirit licenses $6,865,397; land revenue $366,367; stamps (commercial) $298,134; post office $554,240; port and harbour dues $273,918; fees of office $293,063; district collections $176,626; and pawnbrokers $252,774.

During the same year, the main items of expenditure were salaries $2,602,634 ; other charges $1,707,773 ; military expenditure $1,985,508 ; public works $171,009 ; works and buildings (special) $2,157,938 ; roads, streets and bridges (special) $235,095. The expenditure (exclusive of land sales) slightly exceeded the revenue, but the balance to the credit of the Colony was close on $2,500,000.

CHAPTER III.

General Description of the Town and Environs.

APPROACHING Singapore from the West, travellers find themselves in a channel thickly studded with islands, as they reach the southern end of the Straits of Malacca. On the right is to be seen the mountainous group of islands called the Karimons; and further on amongst a number of small islands stands the Raffles Light-house* which guides ships to the old channel of entrance to Singapore Harbour. On the west is Pulau Bukum, a great store place for petroleum and liquid fuel, connected with the town by a cable.

Sailing ships and occasionally steamers coming southward through the Straits of Malacca make use of the old channel. They steer from the Pulau Pisang Light to the Raffles Light-house, and then pass by St. John's Island to the harbour. The P. & O. S. N. Co.'s steamers and others pass between the Sultan Shoal, marked by beacons, on the left, and the Sultan Shoal, marked by a light-house on the right, and thence steam into Keppel Harbour. There is also a light-house on Pulau Pisang, 30 miles outside the western entrance.

On the left, there stretches away to the horizon in a series of undulating hills, the Island of Singapore,

---

*Raffles Light-house, finished in 1855, had a new light put in in 1906, and stands on Coney Island, 13 miles south-west of Singapore Town, in Lat 1° 9′ N., and Long. 103° 44′ 30″ E., group flash white, three in quick succession every ten seconds. Lens, Dioptric of third order. Height of light-house from high water to centre of lens, 106 ft.

with some of the mountains of Johore visible in the distance, notably the conical peak called Gunong Pulai.

The scenery has a quiet beauty that impresses every spectator; and as the water in the channel is generally smooth, all are able to enjoy the prospect. Every now and then the ship startles a gar-fish that skips nimbly over the surface of the water to a safe distance. Occasionally a golden-coloured watersnake may be seen hurrying away from the bows. In the early morning, or afternoon, the sea-eagle may be descried at a great height overhead, watching for its finny prey in the blue waters below. At low-tide vast shoals of coral can be seen in the neighbourhood of the islands in the Strait. If the sun is shining, a curious optical illusion strikes the spectator,—the distant islands seem to be suspended in the air a few feet above the sea. This is probably due to the effect of the sun's rays on the shallow water covering the coral reefs that surround the islands.

One can see from the steamer, as it passes the islands, small Malay fishing kampongs (*i.e.*, villages) with clumps of cocoanut palms overhanging them, and fishing stakes running out into the sea. The method of fishing is ingenious. A long line of stakes, on which a net is hung, is run out to sea for a few hundred yards, ending in a cleverly-arranged *cul-de-sac*. The fish, stopped in their progress by the long line of stakes, swim alongside of it till they find themselves entrapped in the *cul-de-sac*, from which they are transferred at low tide into the fisherman's boat.

As the steamer approaches the harbour, the island seen in front is Pulau Blakang Mati on which the

Artillery barracks are plainly visible at a considerable distance. The entrance to Keppel Harbour lies between Blakang Mati and the Island of Singapore,* and here the steamer passes under the guns of Fort Siloso on the right, and Fort Passir Panjang on the left. Immediately after passing these, Keppel Harbour Dock comes into sight, behind which rises Mount Faber, on which there is a Signal Station and the Observatory for the Time Ball, which gives the time for regulating ships' chronometers. The P. & O. S. N. Co.'s wharf is then reached, opposite to which is the island of Pulau Brani, where a company of Royal Engineers is stationed, and where there are also the large tin-smelting works of the Straits Trading Co.

The mail steamers of the Norddeutscher Lloyd Co. and of the Compagnie des Messageries Maritimes berth at the Borneo wharf, and other steamers from the west at the Tanjong Pagar wharf; both of which are nearer to town than the P. & O. Wharf.

***

Approaching Singapore from the east, ships, after crossing the Gulf of Siam, sight the Horsburgh Light-house,† which stands between Cape Romania and the island of Bintang. (The former disputes with Tanjong Bolus the honour of being the southernmost point of Asia: the latter is a Dutch possession, on which stands the sea-port of Rhio,—or Riouw, according to the Dutch spelling—which was intended

*The Western Harbour limit is marked by a white obelisk on the site of a rock called Lot's wife, which was blown up some time ago. The obelisk is at Berlayer Point, and behind it a gallery is cut in the rock to receive quick-firing guns.

† See note on p. 12.

to be the chief *entrepôt* for trade in the Archipelago. The opening of the Overland Route and, later, of the Suez Canal, and the consequent discontinuance of the Sunda Strait as the passage from Europe to China and Japan has prevented the hopes of its founders from being fulfilled.)

After rounding Cape Romania the long, low-lying Island of Singapore comes into view, behind which are to be seen the distant mountains of the Peninsula, while the channel in front is studded with many small islands. As the ship passes Tanjong Katong,* a long beach above which sea-side bungalows peep through groves of cocoanut palms, the city and roadstead of Singapore appear, the latter crowded with ships of all nations. Bukit Timah, the highest point in the island, Government Hill, Fort Canning, Mount Faber, and the Cathedral spire are the most prominent landmarks, while the tower of the Victoria Memorial Hall (erected in 1905) is a conspicuous object; the general effect of the landscape is very pleasing. Steamers making for the wharves pass through the Roads, and give passengers the opportunity of gaining a fair idea of the situation and general appearance of this picturesque eastern town.

***

The main business part of the town is compactly built on a level stretch of land between Fort Canning and the sea-shore. Part of the plain on which the

* The word Tanjong is literally "land's end," it is a contraction of Tanah hujong, and means a promontory or spit of land. Katong is "turtle," so that Tanjong Katong means "the Turtle Promontory." Its long sandy beach and bathing facilities make it a favourite watering place for the residents. A bar of sand at some distance from the shore protects bathers from the sharks that abound in these waters. A white obelisk about the middle of the beach marks the Eastern Harbour limit.

town is built has been reclaimed from tidal swamps, and part was originally covered by small hills which have been cut away, and their sites are now occupied by streets and squares. Collyer Quay, facing the sea, Battery Road, Commercial Square, or Raffles Place, and the streets leading into it, form the nucleus of the business activity of the town. In this quarter are all the Banks, the Exchange, the offices of the principal European and other merchants and lawyers, the Post Office and the Shipping Office. The trend of expansion is to the westward, to the large reclamation of Teluk Ayer, at the base of Fort Palmer. Many fine offices are built here, the Telegraph Office, and most of the Consulates, lying in a cluster to the north of the Town Market. On the other side of the Singapore River (the north side), stand the Government offices, the Supreme Court, the Town Hall, the Victoria Memorial Hall, the chief Hotels, the English and Roman Catholic Cathedrals, the chief Schools, and for some distance along the sea-shore, there stretches a well laid out Esplanade and Recreation ground, a favourite afternoon resort of residents. Beyond Raffles Hotel extends the part of the town most frequented by non-Chinese inhabitants, with busy Clyde Terrace Market.

Between Tanjong Pagar and the commercial centre of the town lies the Chinese quarter,* in which are the Central Police Station, the Magistrates' Courts, and the Chinese Protectorate. (*See* Chapter V.)

---

* The Chinese population is not confined to this quarter, but is scattered over the whole town. The largest body of Chinese, however, is settled there. Depôts for the accommodation of the endless stream of Chinese immigrants are licensed by Government in this district.

Between the Esplanade and the Rochor River is the district of Kampong Glam, inhabited mainly by Malays and Arabs. The chief European dwellings are built on the north of the town, and extend for several miles into the country. Here, there are a number of small wooded hills, on each of which there are several houses, which are, by reason of their position, airy and well-drained, and therefore healthy and comfortable. On one of the highest of these hills, surrounded by tastefully laid-out grounds, stands Government House, the official residence of the Governor of the Straits Settlements. The roads in this district are well kept; they are skirted by lofty trees, which, often meeting overhead, throw a cool and grateful shade below.

The town of Singapore has three main arteries or thoroughfares, running parallel to the shore. Robinson Road, Collyer Quay, the Esplanade and Beach Road, skirt the shore, crossing the Singapore River by the Cavenagh Bridge. Farther inland, and parallel to it is the long street known on one side of the Singapore River as South Bridge Road, and on the other as North Bridge Road, the two being connected by the Elgin Bridge. The third is that called at different points of its course New Bridge Road, Hill Street and Victoria Street, and is carried over the Singapore River by Coleman Bridge. Each thoroughfare is considerably over two miles in length; and the three form, as it were, the framework upon which the town is built. At right angles to these thoroughfares, four main roads run inland; the first of which, Havelock Road—to begin from the south—skirts the south bank of the Singapore River for the first mile or so of its course, and thence curves round in the direction of

Bukit Chermin and Passir Panjang.* The second, River Valley Road, winds along the north side of the river to Mount Echo and Tanglin; European residences are closely built on both sides of it for a considerable distance. The third, which starting from the Esplanade is called Stamford Road, and from Fort Canning onwards is called Orchard Road, is the chief thoroughfare to the European dwelling houses in the Tanglin district. This is one of the most beautiful roads to be seen anywhere; in one part of its course it is straight for nearly a mile; and one seeing it for the first time cannot fail to be delighted with the long vista of high trees with their variegated foliage and cool shade. If the pigeon-orchid, which grows on most of the trees, happens to be in flower, the pleasure is enhanced.

The fourth road, fourteen miles in length, crosses the island to Kranji, whence the passage to the Sultanate of Johore is made by boats or the railway ferry. It passes the foot of the highest hill in the island—Bukit Timah (Hill of Tin), and is therefore called the Bukit Timah Road. Three other roads cross the island—Thomson Road, branching off the Bukit Timah Road about 2 miles from town, and reaching the Johore Strait at Selitar; Gaylang Road which crosses the eastern part of the island to Changi, and is the main road to Tanjong Katong; and Serangoon Road, which ends some seven miles out on the bank of the Serangoon River. Coast roads to the west, past Keppel Harbour and Passir Panjang; to the east, past Tanjong Katong and Bedoh are in course of construction. There are

* It is called Alexandra Road after the curve.

also a number of charming cross roads in the country, accessible to the bicyclist and by carriage. The Buona Vista Road, from Passir Panjang, rises over the western hills, through the Gap, and furnishes a magnificent view of the seascape to the western side of the island.

For quiet but effective beauty these roads are often compared to the Devonshire lanes. Both Orchard Road and River Valley Road, not to mention others, present the appearance of a well-shaded avenue to an English mansion. The comparison has often been made, but the best that northern latitudes can produce cannot be compared with the richness and variety of the tropical foliage, and the bright colours of the flowering trees. There are many beautiful walks and drives in the environs of Singapore, for a description of which see Chapter IV.

The streets of the town are crowded and busy at all hours of the day, and in the native quarters at nearly all hours of the night as well. Carriages, hack-gharries, bullock-carts, and jinrikishas pass and re-pass in a continual stream; native vendors of various kinds of foods, fruits, and drinks, take up their position by the roadsides, or, wandering up and down the streets proclaim the excellence of their wares; carriers and messengers come and go: all is bustle and activity.

In half-an-hour's walk, a stranger may hear the accents of almost every language and see the features and costume of nearly every race in the world. Amongst the crowds that pass him, he may see, besides Europeans of every nation, Chinese, Malays, Hindus, Madrassees, Sikhs, Japanese, Burmese,

Siamese, Javanese, Boyanese, Singhalese, Tamils, Arabs, Jews, Parsees, Negroes, &c., &c.

At anchor in the Roads, there may be seen any day the ships of all nations, from the Chinese junk to the man-of-war, and gliding in and out among these, or waiting for goods or passengers by the shore, a large flotilla of tongkangs and sampans, manned by Malay, Kling and Chinese boatmen.

The native bazaars both in the centre and on the outskirts of the town always present a lively scene, though their busiest hours are between six and seven in the morning, especially in the suburbs. The visitor to Singapore will do well to stroll round some of the native quarters; and if he be a curio-hunter, he is recommended to inspect the native shops in High Street, which is close to the Hôtel de l'Europe and in streets in the neighbourhood, if he bears in mind that the price asked for an article there is usually treble the amount that will ultimately be accepted.* While High Street is the district *par excellence* for curio-hunting, the more venturesome traveller will take a guide (if he do not understand Malay) and wander along North Bridge Road towards Rochor. The pawn-shops and second-hand dealers thereabout are a revelation as to what articles constitute native wealth.

***

Singapore Island is drained by a number of small streams, dignified by the name of rivers.

---

* The unwary passenger is considered fair game for the native dealer. The present writer was in a shop one day, pricing an article for which the seller demanded $4. Thinking the price too high, he tried to beat it down and said that he was not a passenger but a resident. "O no, sah: I know, sah" said the native. "If you had been passenger, *I ask fifteen dollah, sah.*" And he probably would have got it.

Flowing into the Singapore Strait are:—

1. Jurong River, 10 miles west of the town;
2. Singapore River, passing through the centre of the town;
3. The Rochor, Kalang and Gaylang Rivers, which meet in a large basin at Tanjong Rhu, nearly 2 miles to the east of the town.

Flowing into the Johore Strait are:—

4. The Kranji;
5. The Selitar;
6. The Ponggol;
7. The Serangoon;
8. The Tampinis;
9. The Changi.

The Kranji and Selitar rivers drain the largest extent of country: but the Singapore and Rochor Rivers, with large tidal basins, are navigable for some distance by native craft of considerable size. Crocodiles used to abound in these rivers, and there are still many, especially in the streams on the north of the island; but they are very shy, and are seldom seen.

CHAPTER IV.

FAVOURITE WALKS AND DRIVES.

THE walks and drives about Singapore have a charm peculiarly their own. To those who in a few short weeks have passed through many varieties of scenery—in particular, the sandy wastes that skirt the Suez Canal and Red Sea, and the "barren rocks of Aden"—the soft beauty of the Singapore landscapes is at once refreshing and delightful: and, as there are many visitors who have only a few hours at their disposal in passing through, this chapter is intended to help them to make the best use of their time. When the steamer stays in port for four or five hours, the following drives are recommended, as shewing not only the general appearance of the town but also the beauties of the country roads.*

1.—From the Wharves to Singapore Town and thence to the Botanical Gardens, viâ the Esplanade and Orchard Road.

Passengers land at the P. & O. S. N. Co.'s Wharf (Teluk Blangah†), at the Borneo Wharf, or at the Tanjong Pagar Wharf‡, and to get to the Gardens

---

* The Malay names of the places are added in brackets, for the syces do not understand the English names. The word *Pergi* (pronounce "piggy") means "drive to": e.g. "*pergi Singapura*" or "*pergi ka Singapura*" means "drive to Singapore."

Passengers staying a few days in the island will find the "Malay Pronouncing Hand-Book" (published by Fraser & Neave, Limited), a very useful *vade mecum*. It may be had from booksellers in Singapore and Penang; its price is $1-50.

† Pronounce *Tulloh Blang-ah*.

‡ The syces understand Borneo Wharf and Tanjong Pagar Wharf.

must drive through the town. There is more than one road to town from all the wharves, but the best is that skirting the shore, because of the cool breeze from the sea, and also because the road leads straight to the business part of the town. The syce must be instructed, if this route be chosen, to *Jalan tepi laut** (*i.e.*, to drive by the sea-shore). It is a well-kept road, laid with tramway lines, and the sea is kept in sight most of the way, a distance of three miles, from the P. & O. Wharf. It skirts a number of small laterite hills which are being fast quarried away for road-making purposes. Then Fort Palmer is passed on the right and the Chinese Quarter on the left; and the business part of the town is entered when Robinson Road is reached. Collyer Quay is then entered,—an imposing terrace of offices with the convexity of the curve fronting the sea. At one end is the Teluk Ayer Fish Market, and at the other Johnston's Pier, whence communication is made by boat with the shipping in the Roadstead. The fine building of the Hongkong and Shanghai Banking Corporation is opposite the Pier. From Collyer Quay the passenger enters a triangular space at the junction of Collyer Quay, Battery Road and Flint Street, having on his right the Singapore Club and the Exchange (in one building), the General Post Office and the Shipping Office, behind which is the Volunteer Drill Hall, and the Marine Office. These used to be on the sea wall before the reclamation was made from Johnston's Pier to the river mouth. In front of the Club is a large fountain presented to the Municipality by the late Mr. Tan Kim Seng, a wealthy Chinese citizen. The Chartered Bank is at

* Pronounce *Jahlan tippy lowt.*

the eastern end of Battery Road, which is lined with fine offices and godowns (stores), and leads to Raffles Square, in which are the offices of the Mercantile Bank of India, Ltd., the principal retail stores and lawyers' offices.

Passing on, the visitor crosses the Singapore River by the Cavenagh Bridge to the Esplanade. To the left are the Government offices and Council Chamber, the Town Hall (distinguished by a monument in front, on the top of which is a bronze elephant, erected to commemorate the first visit of the King of Siam to Singapore), the Victoria Memorial Hall and the Supreme Court. Beyond these lies the Esplanade (*Padang Besar**) a large plain, encircled by a well-laid-out carriage drive. The Singapore Cricket Club and the Singapore Recreation Club divide the plain between them for the purpose of cricket, tennis, hockey, football, bowls, and other athletic sports, and in the centre stands a fine statue of Sir T. Stamford Raffles, erected in 1887. A large part of the Esplanade occupies ground reclaimed from the sea; and it is a favourite afternoon resort of the residents. On the landward side are the Hotel de l'Europe, the Municipal Offices (called by the natives *chukei pintu* (door-tax literally) and St. Andrew's Cathedral (*Greja Besar*†). Beach Road goes eastward by the sea shore to the district of Kampong Glam, ending at the Rochor River, but the road now to be taken (Stamford Road) turns inland, and runs straight towards Fort Canning (*Bukit Bandera*‡), passing on the right, first the

---

* Pronounce *Padang Bissar* (*i.e.* The Large Plain).
† Pronounce *Grayja Bissar* (*i.e.* The Large Church).
‡ Pronounce *Bookit Bandayra* (lit. The Hill of the Flags).

Photo by G. R. Lambert & Co.]

CAVENAGH BRIDGE.

Raffles Institution, a school for boys, founded by Sir Stamford Raffles in the year 1823, and then the Church of the Good Shepherd (French Catholic); after which it turns northwards, and from this point is called Orchard Road. The Raffles Library and Museum (*Tempat Kitab**) on the left, is first passed. It is well worth a visit, for the Library is one of the largest and most comprehensive in the East, and the Museum, which is being daily enriched by zoological, mineralogical, ethnological and archæological collections from the Peninsula and the Archipelago, promises to be, in time, one of the finest exhibitions of its kind in Asia. The Reading Room and Museum are open to the public daily (Sunday excepted) from 9-30 a.m. to 6 p.m. There is a valuable collection of Oriental literature, called the Logan Library, access to which may be obtained by special permission from the Librarian. An enlargement is now being made.

Almost opposite the Museum is the Ladies Lawn Tennis Club (*Padang Kechil*)† a prettily laid out garden where tennis is played from 4.30 p.m. till dusk. On the other side of the road lie the new Y. M. C. A. building and Presbyterian Church (*Greja Kechil*) built in 1878; and a little farther on the same side, is a small Hindoo temple, used chiefly by the Dhobies (or washermen) who live in the neighbourhood, and who may be seen at work at any time of the day. Two hundred yards further on, the Jewish Cemetery is to be seen, on the left, opposite Kelly & Walsh's Printing Works. The gate of the approach to Government House is then passed on the right, beyond which is Koek's Bazaar, a row of native shops on both sides of

* Pronounce *T'mpat Kitab* (*i.e.* The Place of Books).
† Pronounce *Padang Kitchy* (*i.e.* The Little Plain).

the road. Between the hours of six and eight in the morning, this market presents a lively scene ; hundreds of Chinese cooks and Asiatic women of many various nationalities come at that hour to make their purchases for the day.

Beyond the Bazaar, near which the railway crosses the road by an overhead bridge, Orchard Road becomes a straight, well-shaded drive, leading to the European residences in the Tanglin district. On the left, almost hidden by the trees is a very large Chinese Burial Ground formerly used by the Teo Chews, *i.e.*, Chinese hailing from Swatow. The visitor may perhaps overtake a funeral on its way to one of these Chinese burying grounds in the suburbs, with the customary accompaniments of gongs to startle, and the scattering of gold and silver paper to appease the demons which are supposed to be on the watch for the spirit of the deceased. Orchard Road ends at the entrance to the Military Barracks in Tanglin : and turning to the right into Napier Road, the visitor soon finds himself at the gate of the Botanical Gardens (*Kebun Bungah*).*

These gardens were opened in the year 1873 ; and they are kept up by the Straits Government. Many varieties of tropical trees and flowers are to be seen there. In one of the ponds, the *Victoria Regia* spreads its broad leaves over the water. There is a large variety of orchids and tropical ferns in the orchid houses ; and close to these used to be a small zoological collection of birds, snakes, and a few wild animals.

---

* Pronounce *K'boon Boong-ah (i.e.* Garden of Flowers).

Photo by G. R. Lambert & Co.]

VIEW IN BOTANICAL GARDENS.

On a hill to the north-west of the Gardens stands Tyersall, the Singapore residence of His Highness the Sultan of Johore. To the west are situated the barracks, with golf links, the parade ground, and in a hollow behind, a rifle range.

2.—From the Wharves to the Impounding Reservoir viâ Singapore Town.

The Reservoir (*Kolam Ayer**) from which is drawn the water-supply of the town, is rather more than four miles to the north of the city. The route from the Wharves is the same as described above as far as the Ladies' Lawn Tennis Club, leaving which on the left, the passenger drives along Selegie Road, where there is a dense population of Eurasians and natives, till the Rochor River is reached, along the left bank of which for some distance runs the Bukit Timah Road. Turning into this road the visitor passes along the foot of Sophia Hill, and Government Hill (on the left) between the summits of which is the High Level Reservoir. The Pumping Station stands about 60 feet below. On the right the road passes, at some distance, the Race Course, where half-yearly Race Meetings and occasional Gymkhanas are held. It is used also as a Golf Course by the Singapore Golf Club, which was founded in 1891. A little further on the road runs between the filter beds on the left and the Christian Cemetery (*Kuboran Orang Puteh*†) on the right. The burying space is divided between the Roman Catholics and the Protestants, and two Mortuary Chapels stand at either side of the entrance. Turn-

* Pronounce *Kolam Ire (i.e.* Pond of Water).

† Pronounce *Kooboran Orang Pooty* (*i.e.*, The burial place of the whitemen.)

ing to the right at the cross roads the Red Bridge (*Jembatan Merah*) marks the commencement of Thomson Road, and after a drive of nearly two miles along this well-shaded road the visitor arrives at the Impounding Reservoir. It is a small lake, about a mile-and-a-half long in the heart of the jungle, the water being retained at the lower end by an extensive dam. To the right stands a bunaglow belonging to the Municipality. To the left runs a road which ends about a mile further on at the shore of the lake. The reservoir is one of the prettiest spots on the island; at sunset or by moonlight it is perhaps seen at its best. Tiger-tracks are occasionally to be seen in the neighbourhood, this being the nearest place to the town where tigers have been traced or killed in recent years.

3.—From the Wharves to Johore Bahru.

If the traveller have a little longer time, anything above five hours, he cannot do better than cross the island by the Singapore-Kranji Railway and thence to Johore. The Railway was opened in 1903, and before that, the trip to Johore was done by carriage, the road being a good one, and the journey giving an excellent idea of the interior of the island. The main Railway Station is at the back of Fort Canning (the gharry syce should be told *pergi kreta api*). Eight trains run daily each way, and the time table is published in the local newspapers. The journey by train occupies a little over an hour and ends at Woodlands Station on the Johore Straits, whence a steam ferry takes the traveller to Johore, where there is an excellent hotel and plenty to see for several hours.

Leaving Singapore Station, the line curves through a cutting to the left of Orchard Road, crosses that thoroughfare by a bridge and cuts through Emerald Hill, whence it emerges on the Bukit Timah Road, beyond the Cemetery. Newton is the first station. The Railway then runs straight across the plain, parallel with a small river and the Bukit Timah road, passing Cluny and Holland Road Stations, to the foot of Bukit Timah—the Hill of Tin, 519 feet in height and the highest point in the island.

The ascent of this hill is made by carriage or on foot. There is a Government Bungalow on the summit, to which residents go occasionally for a change of air. There are two Mission Chapels in the Bukit Timah district, for Chinese converts. One belongs to the English Presbyterian Mission; the other, the Chapel of St. Joseph, to the French Catholic Mission (*Missions Etrangères*).

Winding round the foot of this beautifully wooded eminence, the train goes through gambier, pepper, and pineapple plantations, beside grass-covered and verdure-clad hills, past Bukit Panjang Station, to Woodlands, the terminus on the Strait of Johore.

The Johore Strait (*Silat Tebrau*), varying from three-quarters of a mile to two miles in breadth, thickly wooded on both sides to the water's edge, charms the visitor with beauties that are peculiar to land and water scenery; the ever changing light and shade throw the landscape into combinations of colour that are as pleasing as they are varied. Travellers have compared it favourably with the

Rhine scenery, with Loch Lomond, and with the best views on the estuaries of the Forth and the Tay.

Johore Bahru ("New Johore") the capital of the dominions of the Sultan of Johore (which includes Muar) is a town with a population of 20,000. The chief place of interest is the Istana, or palace, which faces the Strait.

The handsome Johore Hotel first strikes the visitor on landing. It is equal in accommodation to any in Singapore, is beautifully situated, and if the precaution be taken to telephone across, will supply even a very large party with breakfast, tiffin or dinner. The Johore Civil Service Club has quarters in the hotel. The Istana is to the west of the hotel; the native town to the east. Permission may usually be obtained to see over the former, but its treasures of gold and silver plate and the Throne Room, can only be seen by special permission. The curious traveller will visit the native town and watch the gambling, which is here permitted by license to Chinese.

The hinterland of Johore is now being opened up by a railway extending from Johore Bahru north-westerly to join the Federated States Railway beyond Mount Ophir, the prominent mountain (3,690 feet) noted by steamship passengers while going through the Straits of Malacca near that place. It is the last link of the chain stretching from the mainland opposite Penang, to the Wharves at Singapore, and also—so says the optimist—the southern section of the railway, that will eventually run through Kedah and Burma to India, and eventually to Europe.

There are a few bungalows at various places in the island, at which residents and others may enjoy a short period of country life; some are the property of the Government, and others are let by private individuals.

The bungalows let by the Government are:—

1. Changi Bungalow, at the eastern extremity of the island, 14 miles from town. There is good sea bathing to be had here.

2. Bukit Timah Bungalow on the hill of that name.

3. Selitar Bungalow, nine miles from town, on the Thomson Road. Here there is an excellent fresh-water swimming-bath.

These bungalows are rented (furnished) to the general public, preference being given to Government servants and military officers.

Other bungalows, belonging to private individuals, are to be had on the sea-shore at Passir Panjang to the west, and Tanjong Katong to the east of the town. At both places there is good sea-bathing.

CHAPTER V.

PUBLIC BUILDINGS AND PLACES OF INTEREST.

BOTANICAL GARDENS.

(Malay Name.—*Kebûn Bûnga*).

ONE of the favourite resorts of residents and visitors are these gardens, situated about three miles from town. They are managed by the Government Director of Gardens and Forests (H. N. Ridley, Esq., F.L.S.), assisted by a committee of local gentlemen. Before they were taken up by Government, the Gardens were maintained by local subscriptions; and when the idea of having public Gardens was first conceived, part of the slope of Fort Canning Hill was utilized for the purpose, until the ground where the Gardens now are was obtained. Government took over the Gardens in December, 1874. They occupy a large extent of ground on and around a hill between the Infantry Barracks at Tanglin and Tyersall, the Singapore residence of H. H. the Sultan of Johore. A great variety of tropical plants and trees may be seen in the grounds; there are several ferneries and orchid houses; beyond the band stand is a pretty valley devoted to palms. To the right the visitor may obtain a good idea of what tropical vegetation is, a strip being left as near primeval jungle as possible. There used to be on the shoulder of the hill, a small aviary

Photo by G. R. Lambert & Co.

ENTRANCE TO BOTANICAL GARDENS.

and monkey-house where specimens of some of the rarer birds, beasts and reptiles of the Straits and neighbourhood were on exhibition. (*See* also p. 42.)

The grounds are well-laid out, and the beauty of the landscape, as well as the interest of the botanical collection make this one of the most attractive spots in Singapore to both residents and visitors. Close by are the Experimental Forest Nurseries, opened in 1884, between Cluny and Dalvey Roads.

BOUSTEAD INSTITUTE.

A handsome building, at the corner of Anson Road and Tanjong Pagar Road. It is intended for the benefit of Seamen. It is three storeys high; and fitted with bedrooms, refreshment rooms, recreation rooms of various kinds and a hall for meetings. The Institute was founded by the executors of the late Edward Boustead, Esq., who left a large sum of money for charitable purposes.

BUKIT TIMAH.

This hill, the highest point in Singapore Island, stands at an elevation of 519 feet above the sea-level. There is a Government Bungalow on the summit, from which a magnificent view of Singapore, the islands in the Singapore Strait, and the southern part of the Malay Peninsula, can be obtained on a clear day. There is a carriage road all the way to the bungalow; while there are short cuts which may be taken by pedestrians. Formerly, the jungle on the hill was infested by tigers; traces of them are occasionally found even now, but rarely. One or two disused pits dug by the natives to entrap these animals may be seen here and there upon the hill.

Visitors to Singapore, who have about six hours to spare, will find themselves amply repaid by an excursion to the top of Bukit Timah, alighting at the Railway Station of that name; there are few finer views to be had anywhere in the world. The distance from the Station to the summit is about two miles and is a good walk.

BUKIT TIMAH CEMETERY.

(Malay Name.—*Kubôran Orang Puteh*).

Two miles from town, on the Bukit Timah Road, is the Christian Cemetery, opened nearly thirty years ago, when the old burial-ground on Fort Canning Hill was disused. The Cemetery is divided between the Roman Catholics and Christians of other denominations; the Catholic portion with its mortuary chapel is on the left as one enters the gate, the Protestant section and mortuary chapel are on the right. The new Christian Cemetery is between the 3rd and 4th mile on the Serangoon Road.

CHINESE PROTECTORATE.

As the name implies, this is the office of the Protector of Chinese, whose duties are to attend to the interests of Chinese residents and immigrants, especially the latter. The building is a plain and unpretentious one, and stands in Havelock Road not far from its junction with New Bridge Road.*

* The establishment of a Chinese Protectorate was first advised in the 1875 Report of the Inspector-General of Police, to be under "a European conversant with some dialect of Chinese, &c." Ordinance III. of 1877, the Crimping Ordinance, allows the appointment of Protector of Immigrants. Mr. W. A. Pickering, C.M.G., was the first who held the appointment. He resigned office in 1888. It ought to be stated that the main object of the Protector of Chinese is to protect the ignorant Chinese from their fellow-countrymen.

CHURCHES (*See* Chapter VI).

CLUBS (*See* Chapter VIII).

THE CONVENT OF THE HOLY INFANT JESUS, stands between Victoria Street and North Bridge Road, opposite the Cathedral Church of the Good Shepherd (French Catholic). The Convent was founded in 1854, it has in connection with it an orphanage and girls' school, and a refuge for distressed women, irrespective of race. Both school and orphanage are large and prosperous; it is supported by contributions willingly given by all classes in the community, and draws a monthly grant from Government for the orphanage, in addition to the educational grant made yearly under the Code. The handsome chapel was built in 1903 with funds derived from France.

DOCKS.

The Docks and Wharves (with the exception of the P. & O. Wharf) are controlled by the Tanjong Pagar Dock Board, having been expropriated by the Colonial Government from the Tanjong Pagar Dock Company in 1905. There were originally the Tanjong Pagar Dock Co., controlling the eastern section; and the New Harbour Dock Co., controlling the western section. The latter is the older having been started in 1858, the former in 1864, but the two were amalgamated in 1900. The Tanjong Pagar Dock Board has also a large interest in the Singapore Slipway and Engineering Co.

The Tanjong Pagar Section has wharves a mile-and-a-quarter in length, lying to the south-west of the city, with which they are connected by electric tramways. The extension of the Singapore-Kranji Railway from the former terminus at the foot of

Fort Canning runs at the back of the hill near the entrance to Tanjong Pagar Dock and thence down alongside the road to Alexandra Road. The following are the particulars of these wharves:—

	Length.	Depth at low water.
West Wharf ..	Over $1\frac{1}{2}$ miles ...	25 to 35 feet.
Sheers do. ...	340 feet ...	26 "
East do. ...	500 "	Outside 25 "
		Inside 16 "

There are two large Graving Docks: the *Victoria Dock*, with a length on the block of 450 feet, breadth of entrance 65 feet, and depth of water on sill at ordinary spring tides 20 feet; and the *Albert Dock*, with a length on the block of 475 feet, breadth of entrance 60 feet, and depth of water on sill at ordinary spring tides 21 feet. There are large and well-fitted machine shops, &c., on the Wharf, with all materials for the rapid refitting of ships; there are extensive godowns for the reception and storage of cargo; and coal sheds, roofed with corrugated iron, capable of holding 100,000 tons of coal stand immediately behind the Wharf. Ships are coaled by Chinese coolies with an astonishing rapidity.

The Keppel Harbour Section, originally started in 1858, as the Patent Slip and Dock Co., has two graving docks, a large wharf, a machine shop, foundries and godowns for cargo and coal. No. 1 Dock has a length of 375 feet, breadth of entrance 42 feet, and depth of water on sill at ordinary spring tides 14 to $15\frac{1}{2}$ feet: the corresponding measurements of No. 2 Dock are 459 feet, 62 feet and 19 to 20 feet respectively.

The Singapore Slipway and Engineering Company

have two slipways at Tanjong Rhu, on the N.E. side of the town. No. 1, 429 feet long, takes up vessels of 500 tons; No. 2, with a length of 200 feet, can accommodate vessels up to 50 tons.

ESPLANADE.

(Malay Name.—*Padang Besár*).

This is a large plain skirting the sea, in the heart of the city. About fifteen acres of lawn, round which runs a broad and well-made carriage drive, are railed off for purposes of recreation, and are divided between the Singapore Cricket Club and the Singapore Recreation Club. The Singapore Cricket Club, which occupies the part nearest to the Singapore River, has a large and well-appointed pavilion at one end of the Esplanade, while the Singapore Recreation Club has a smaller pavilion at the other. In the middle of the plain is a statue of Sir Stamford Raffles. Cricket, tennis, hockey, football and bowls are played on the plain. On the landward side of the Esplanade stand the Hotel de l'Europe, the Municipal Offices, and St. Andrew's Cathedral; and beyond the carriage drive on the other side, is a strip of green along the sea-wall, with a foot-path, which affords a cool and pleasant walk in the early morning and afternoon.

Round the plain and along the sea-wall rows of trees add greatly to the beauty of the scene. There are several very fine Angsana trees, at seasons a glowing mass of bloom.

DRILL HALL.

This large and spacious building designed by Hon. Major McCallum, R.E., C.M.G., the Colonial Engineer, and built by Government for the Singapore Volunteer Artillery in 1891, stands on the site of the original fort on the island—Fort Fullerton—behind the General Post Office and the Shipping Office.*

THE EXCHANGE AND CHAMBER OF COMMERCE.

The Exchange is a handsome building close by Johnston's Pier. It was erected in 1879. The lower floor is occupied by the Chamber of Commerce, and the Exchange. In the hall is a fine bronze bust of General Sir Andrew Clarke, R.E., K.C.M.G., C.B., who was Governor of the Straits Settlements from 1873 to 1875. The upper storey is used by the Singapore Club, and has large tiffin, billiard and reading rooms. At the back of the building, overlooking the sea, there are spacious and cool verandahs.

FORT CANNING.

(Malay Name.—*Bûkit Bandêra*).

Fort Canning Hill stands behind the town, the main approach to it being from Orchard Road. It was originally called Government Hill, because Sir Stamford Raffles fixed his residence there, on his arrival in the island. For more than forty years his house continued the Government residence. The Fort is now used as Artillery Barracks, and on the southern summit of the hill, at a height of 156 feet above the sea level, stands a signal station, and flag staff and a light tower, facing the town and strait. Shipping and fire signals are shewn on the staff, the time gun and salutes are fired from the Fort (*see* p. 24). On the slope of the hill, below the Fort towards the south-east are the Old Cemetery and the shrine of Iskander Khan (*vide infra*). A very fine view of the town and strait is to be had from the battlements of the Fort.

* The Drill Hall is now (1907) being re-erected on Beach Road Reclamation.

GAOL.

The Criminal and Civil Prisons are at Sepoy Lines a little over a mile from the centre of the town. There is accommodation in the Criminal Prison for rather over 1,000 prisoners, and in the Civil Prison for about 130. Within the Criminal Prison, and contained by its own inner wall, is what is now known as the Old Prison, built as a Civil Prison in 1847, the Criminal Prison being then in a different part of the town. This continued in use as a Civil Prison until 1902, the Criminal Prison being built round it in 1882. The present Civil Prison adjoins the Criminal Prison but is separate from it. There are 45 European Warders and about 50 native sub-warders for the two prisons.

GOVERNMENT HOUSE.

(Malay Name.—*Tûan Gubenor pûnya Rûmah*).

On the top of what is now called Government Hill and in the midst of a spacious and beautifully laid-out park stands Government House, which both for situation and architecture is perhaps the finest building of its kind in the Far East. The site and grounds cost more than $40,000, and the cost of the building itself was $180,000. Before its erection and occupation, the residence of the Governor was on Fort Canning and afterwards on Leonie Hill in Grange Road. Singapore owes the present Government House to Major-General Sir Harry St. George Ord, the first Governor of the Colony after its transference from the Indian Government to the Crown. His proposals were at first received with disfavour, the popular impression being that a building of that size and expense was unnecessary and extravagant. More recently, however, it has been found that Government House, large as it is, is not nearly large enough to meet local requirements particularly on such an occasion as the King's Birthday Ball. The plans for the building were drawn up by Major McNair, R.A., and the house was ready for occupation in 1869. The architecture is of a composite order; Doric and Ionic elements being, however, most prominent. The length of frontage is 235 feet, and the width of the main building is 73 feet. In the centre, above the entrance-hall rises a tower crowned with a Mansard roof. A wing at the back runs at right angles to the main building, over 100 feet in length. The wide verandahs, on both storeys, give one the impression that the internal accommodation of the edifice is larger than it really is. Entering at the main door, through the porch, the visitor finds himself in a large marble-paved hall, opening on the left into a long dining room, with a small billiard-room screened off at the far end; and on the right into the ball-room, at the far end of which is a fine statue of Her Majesty Queen Victoria unveiled in the Jubilee Year (1887). In front of him, there is a wide staircase leading to the reception room on the upper floor. The interior is tastefully furnished, and the whole building was fitted with electric light in 1890. The main approach to Government House is from Orchard Road, where, passing through massive iron gates, a carriage drive (formerly called Edinburgh Road) winds up the hill through the domain to the house. From the top of the hill there is an extensive view of the town and strait, and a large part of the island.

GOVERNMENT OFFICES.

(Malay Name.—*Second Gubenor pûnya Ofis*).

These stand on the north bank of the Singapore river, near Cavenagh Bridge, all included in one large building. In this building are included the Secretariat, the Audit Office, the Registry of Deeds, the Land Office, the Public Works and Medical Departments, the Treasury and Stamp Office, the Education Office and the Offices of the Colonial Engineer, the Official Assignee, and the Attorney General. The original building was much smaller than the present one, but considerable additions were made in 1879 and 1888, the whole of the wing at the rear being erected in the last-named year. The Treasure-room is a strongly built detached structure on the river side of the Public Offices.

The Council Chamber, in the centre of the building on the upper floor, is a spacious room, in the middle of which, enclosed in an iron railing, is the Council table, at which the Hon. Legislators sit during their deliberations. On the wall, at one end of the hall, hangs a portrait of Her Majesty Queen Victoria in her royal robes; and at the further end of the room is a handsomely carved teak screen.

HOSPITALS (*See* Chapter VI).

HOTELS (*See* Chapter VIII).

LADIES' LAWN OR DHOBY GHAUT.

(Malay Name.—*Padang Kechil*).

Originally called Dhoby Ghaut, the plot of ground opposite the Scotch Church, in Orchard Road, is now the Ladies' Lawn Tennis Ground, with a pavilion on the further side. There are excellent lawn tennis and croquet courts, which are nicely kept and greatly appreciated.

SHIPPING OFFICE, MARINE DEPARTMENT.

(Malay Name.—*Shahbunder punya Ofis* or *Ofis Khlâsi*).

The old Shipping Office used to stand on the ground now occupied by the rear wing of the Government Offices; but some years ago it was removed to more commodious premises on the south bank of the Singapore river, dividing with the Drill Hall and the General Post Office, the site of Fort Fullerton. The basement of the landward part is occupied by the Import and Export Office, and the upper storey by the Shipping Master. In the seaward portion are the offices of the Master Attendant, Registrar of Shipping, Port Health Officer, and the Marine Court. A small pier across the road along the Reclamation affords accommodation for the Master Attendants' boats and launches.

MARKETS.

There are five large Markets in Singapore:—

1. The Town Market, at the western end of Raffles Quay;
2. Clyde Terrace Market in Beach Road;
3. Ellenborough Market, near New Bridge Road;
4. Rochor Market, in the district of that name; and,
5. Orchard Road Market (Koek's Bazaar), in the road whose name it bears.

The Markets are farmed by the Municipality, that is to say the exclusive right of letting the stalls in these markets is farmed out at an annual rental. Fish, fresh meat, poultry, eggs, fruit, vegetables, and other produce are sold by native vendors at these markets; in the early morning and in the afternoon when the supplies of fresh fish are for sale, the scene at the markets is lively and interesting.

MONUMENTS.

The Dalhousie Obelisk commemorating the first visit of a Governor-General of India to Singapore, stands near the Cricket Pavilion at the S. W. end of the Esplanade. Lord Dalhousie was Governor-General of India from 1848 to 1856, and it was during his administration that he visited Singapore. The monument was removed from its original site—only a few yards from where it now stands—in 1891, because, owing to recent improvements in the Esplanade, its remaining where it was would have impeded the traffic.

In front of the Town Hall stands a monument, —a bronze Elephant on a high pedestal—commemorating the first visit of H. M. Somdech Phra Paramindr Maha Chulalonkorn, King of Siam, to Singapore, in 1871. Inscriptions on the pedestal in English, Chinese, Siamese, and Malay record this fact.

In the middle of the Esplanade there is a fine statue of Sir Thomas Stamford Raffles, the founder of the Settlement, erected in 1887. Sir Stamford is represented in a standing posture, with folded arms, head slightly bent and looking seawards. The pedestal is of grey granite, and bears his coat of arms.

A monument to the late Colonel Ronald Macpherson, R.A., at one time Lieutenant-Governor and Colonial Secretary in the Straits Settlements (*ob.* 1867), stands in the Cathedral Compound, facing the sea. It consists of a pedestal and decorated shaft of grey and red granite, surmounted by a Maltese cross.

Among the monuments there should be included the handsome fountain presented to the town by the late Mr. Tan Kim Seng, a Chinese gentleman, who in other ways proved himself a public benefactor. The occasion of its erection was the completion of the works by which a good water-supply was brought to the town. The fountain stands in Battery Road, opposite the General Post Office and the Exchange.

OLD CEMETERY.

The original burial-ground of the first residents in Singapore is on the slope of Fort Canning Hill. It was opened in 1822, and consecrated by the Bishop of Calcutta in 1834; but was disused on the opening of the new Cemetery in Bukit Timah Road in 1867. Here sleep some of the fathers of the Colony, and many old residents. Two Gothic gate-ways, at the north and south ends, afford an entrance to the burial-ground "where heaves the turf in many a mouldering heap." In spite of care, many of the old tomb stones and monuments are falling to pieces.

The southern half was allotted to members of the Anglican communion, the northern to other Christian denominations.

POLICE COURT AND COURT OF REQUESTS.

The Police Courts—a large and imposing structure—are built at the south end of the Hong Lim Green,* and face South Bridge Road. The build-

* Called after Mr. Hong Lim, a Chinese gentleman, who contributed $4,000 towards its upkeep. The green was originally offered by the Government to the Chinese population as a recreation-ground, on condition that it should be properly kept. Had it not been for the liberality of Mr. Hong Lim, this scheme would have fallen through.

ing is T shaped; its architecture is mainly Corinthian; a Mansard roof crowns the centre. It was erected in 1884. Here sit the Magistrates' and Bench Courts while the Court of Requests (for sums not exceeding $100) is accommodated below the Police Offices.

CENTRAL POLICE STATION.

(Malay Name.—*Rumah Pâsong Besâr*).

Opposite the Police Courts in South Bridge Road. Erected in 1887, and lately rebuilt. A disastrous explosion occurred in the Court yard in 1891, when a detachment of police were engaged in emptying old cartridges. Several constables were killed, and more severely injured. The Central Station is connected by telephone with all the town stations and with most in the country districts.

GENERAL POST OFFICE.

The General Post Office, originally a one-storey pavilion, built in 1874, is now a handsome two-storey building, the addition being made in 1883. It stands between the Exchange and the Master Attendant's Office, on the site of Fort Fullerton. The four corners are surmounted by Mansard roofs; and the general style of the building and its ornamentation is of the Corinthian order.

The interior consists of a large hall, lighted from the roof, and round the hall, below, are the business counters and offices, and above, on the second storey, a gallery into which open other offices.

RACE COURSE.

(Malay Name.—*Pâdang Lomba Kûda*).

The race-course is on a plain to the east of Government Hill, and is approached by the Bukit Timah and Campong Java Roads. The length of the course is one mile 83 yards. The Singapore Sporting Club hold two race meetings annually, in May and October. The spacious Paddock Stables and Grand Stands are on the N. W. side of the course, off Campong Java Road. The course is also used as a golfing links by the Singapore Golf Club. There used to be a rifle range there but it was removed many years ago to Balestier (*see* also p. 64).

RAFFLES INSTITUTION.

(Malay Name.—*Skôla Besár*).

This, the largest educational establishment in the Colony, is in Beach Road, facing the sea. It was founded in 1823, by Sir Stamford Raffles, whose name it bears, and endowed by the Indian Government with large grants of land. The land, however, was given back to the Government in consideration of an annual grant in money. Raffles intended the Institution for the higher education of Asiatics, but his plan was departed from : it is now an elementary English School, with special higher classes for the benefit of intending competitors for the King's Scholarships. (These Scholarships are open annually to boys from any school in the Colony; they are intended to help promising students to complete their education at one or other of the British Universities).

The school, formerly under the management of a Board of Trustees, was taken over by Government in 1903. The Principal is C. M. Phillips, Esq., M.A. LL.B., (*Cantab*).

A Girl's School (Malay Name—*Skôla Missy*) was added to the Institution in 1845. The building is in Bras Basah Road, adjoining the premises of the Boys' School. It is a training school as well as a day school.

Photo by G. R. Lambert & Co.

RAFFLES LIBRARY AND MUSEUM.

RAFFLES LIBRARY AND MUSEUM.

(Malay Name.—*Rûmah Kitab Skola Gambar* or *Tempat Bûk*).

This building was opened in the Jubilee year of Her Majesty Queen Victoria (1887). It stands in Orchard Road, at the foot of Fort Canning Hill. It is a long, narrow edifice, of composite architecture, surmounted by a dome. The original plans, designed by Hon. Major McCallum, R.E., C.M.G., were drawn for a building double the size of the present one, but the expenditure was disallowed by the Colonial Office, so half of the proposed building had to be sacrificed. The basement is occupied by the Library, Reading Room, and Offices; and the upper floor is devoted to the Museum. Part of the building was reserved for the Curator's quarters, but owing to the rapid extension of the Museum, this part was added to the public rooms and offices.

The Library contains about 20,000 volumes; and the Museum is rich in zoological and ethnological specimens connected with Malaysia. The Reading room is open to the public from 9.30 a.m. to 6 p.m. The Institution enjoys an annual grant from Government, and is managed by a Committee, appointed by the Governor, of which the Colonial Secretary is *ex officio* Chairman. An extension was made in 1906. (*See* also p. 41).

RESERVOIRS.

The Mount Emily High Service Reservoir is on an elevation between Government and Sophia Hills. There are two cisterns, holding together about 3,000,000 gallons, into which water is forced by a steam-pump at the foot of the hill. Before being pumped up to the cistern, the water, brought in pipes from the Impounding Reservoir (*vide infra*), passes through the large filter beds in Bukit Timah Road (opened in 1891). The grounds round the High Service Reservoir are laid out as a garden, with flowers, shrubs and trees. A number of garden seats are placed along the foot-paths, and a very fine view, towards the east and north, is to be had on a clear day. The High Service Reservoir at Pearl's Hill, behind the Gaol was completed in 1903. It supplies the southern part of the town.

The Impounding Reservoir (Malay Name—*Kôlam Ayer*) is on the left of Thomson Road four miles from town. (*See* page 43). The Municipality have enlarged it to nearly double its original size, and raised the dam five feet.

RIFLE RANGE, BALESTIER.

(Malay Name.—*Tempat Tembak*).*

On the Balestier plain, behind the Tan Tock Seng Hospital and opposite the Leper Hospital. There are six pairs of targets and a range of 1200 yards. The range is used by the Singapore Rifle Association, the Police and the Volunteers; the Swiss Rifle-Shooting Club have a range of their own, and a handsome Club house at Bukit Tinggi, one of the eastern points of the Bukit Timah range.

SAILORS' HOME.

(Malay Name.—*Rûmah Khlâsi*).

This institution, which is intended to supply board and lodging to seamen on shore, stands at the

---

* Final *k* not sounded.

corner of Stamford Road and North Bridge Road, opposite St. Andrew's Cathedral. It was established in 1851. The charges are :—

For Officers	...	...	$1-75 per diem.
„ Seamen	...	...	0-80 „

ST. ANDREW'S HOUSE.

A Boarding-House for boys in connection with the Church of England. The present building was erected in 1891: it stands at the foot of Fort Canning Hill, in Armenian Street, off Stamford Road.

ST. JOSEPH'S INSTITUTION.

Commonly called the Brothers' School, was founded in 1852, by the French Missionary Society at the instigation of Father Beurel. It is now in a flourishing state, though for five years (1880-1885) it was suspended owing to the want of men to carry on the work. The building with a small chapel attached, stands in Bras Basah Road, almost opposite the Church of the Good Shepherd and was largely extended in 1902. The system of education in the school is on purely secular lines, religious instruction being given, however, to the pupils belonging to the Roman Catholic faith. A number of boys are received as boarders.

SHRINE OF ISKANDER KHAN.

(Malay Name.—*Krâmat Iskander Khan*).

This shrine is on the southern slope of Fort Canning Hill, near the old Cemetery. Crossing part of the old moat by a wooden bridge, the visitor enters the sacred place, and finds himself in a grove of very old and lofty trees, in the centre of which is a stucco-covered tomb, closely railed in. A pan of incense is kept burning at the foot of it day and night; the railing and the trees are covered with the memorials and offerings of the devout. After sunset on Friday and Sunday evenings, crowds of worshippers flock to this place. The shrine is believed to be the resting-place of the Sultan Iskander, one of the heroes of the *Sejârat Malayu*,* on what authority it is hard to say. The tomb was discovered by accident after the British settlement in the island, when the jungle on Fort Canning was being cut away. It is a very holy spot for Mahommedans, and visits to it are supposed to cure diseases. A foot-path close to the southern entrance of the old Christian Cemetery leads to the shrine.

SHRINE OF HABIB NOOR.

(Malay Name.—*Kramât Habib Noor*).

This is a small mausoleum of oriental architecture, which stands on a small knoll at Cursetjee's Corner (Parsee Lodge), near the foot of Mount Palmer. Here was buried a Mahommedan Saint, Habib Noor, who died about half a century ago, after a life which gained a great reputation for sanctity not only in Singapore where he lived, but throughout a large part of Malaysia. A small Malay cemetery lies round the shrine. The approach to it is from Anson Road.

---

* The only English translation of the *Sejârat Maláyu* known to the writer is Leyden's Malay Annals, now out of print. Iskander Khan or Iskander Shah is the Eastern name of Alexander the Great, and seems to have been used as a title for various Mahommedan sovereigns. The Sultans of Singapore always adopted it.

SUPREME COURT.

The Supreme Court is at the south end of High Street, facing the Esplanade. It is a large and airy building, two storeys in height. The architecture is mainly of the Doric order, and the whole structure has a massive appearance. It is surmounted by a small dome and flag-staff. The building as it now stands is an improvement (completed in 1873) of an older building erected in 1832, and again extended in 1901 to accommodate two courts, the Registrar, Bar-room, Library, &c.

TANGLIN BARRACKS.

The Infantry Barracks in the Tanglin district, are about three miles to the N. W. of the town, and stand on an elevation between Mount Echo and the Botanical Gardens. The situation is airy and healthy; the ground enclosed is nearly one square mile in extent, and within the enclosure are the Officers' Bungalows and Men's Quarters, Shops, Magazine, the Parade ground, rifle range (800 yards), and a large amount of open space for recreation and exercise.

ALEXANDRA BARRACKS.

These extensive barracks lie on hills to the west of Alexandra Road and within easy reach of the Mount Faber Range and the western defences of the Fortress.

VICTORIA MEMORIAL AND TOWN HALL.

At the Town end of the Esplanade stands this handsome combined building which is devoted to public purposes in Singapore, and is under the control of the Municipal Commissioners. The original Town Hall was built in 1854 and then consisted of an upper room for concerts, balls, &c., and a lower hall with a small stage that could be used as a theatre. When the Victoria Memorial Hall was completed, the Town Hall was reconstructed, with a facade to harmonise with the new building, the upper and lower halls were thrown into one to form a large and commodious theatre, with side rooms. In the Memorial Hall there are a number of pictures of well-known gentlemen connected with the Straits, including:—

Col. W. J. Butterworth, Governor of Singapore from 1843 to 1855.

Major-General William Orfeur Cavenagh, Governor from 1861 to 1867, painted by public subscription, 1868.

Thomas Scott, Esq. (of Messrs. Guthrie & Co.), presented by the Chinese rate-payers.

Mr. W. H. Read, C.M.G.

General Sir Harry St. George Ord, first Governor of the Straits Settlements after their transfer to the Crown (1867-1873).

Sir Cecil Clementi Smith, G.C.M.G., presented by Mr. Cheang Hong Lim, in 1891.

Admiral of the Fleet, Sir Henry Keppel.

Mr. Thomas Shelford, C.M.G.

Mr. William Adamson, C.M.G.

Sir Charles B. H. Mitchell, K.C.M.G.

The Tower of the Victoria Memorial Hall is a conspicuous object both from the sea and from land. The handsome clock in it, with chimes, is the gift of the Straits Trading Company.

TYERSALL.

(Malay Name.—*Rûmah Maharaja*).

This large and palatial building is the Singapore residence of H. H. the Sultan of Johore. Originally a small country house, it was added to, or rather rebuilt on a much larger scale, in 1892. It stands on the top of a hill near the gardens, in the middle of a well-laid out demesne. Near by is Woodneuk, a favourite stopping place of H. H. the Sultan.

NOTE:—The Malay names of places are not given in cases where the English names are usually understood by the *syces*.

For a list of Malay names of places in common use, and some Malay phrases see Chap. IX.

CHAPTER VI.

Places of Worship and Hospitals.

THE diversity of races in Singapore is made evident to the eye by the many buildings throughout the town and island devoted to the purposes of religion. A list of these follows, with brief descriptions of the principal ones.

1. The Church of England.

St. Andrew's Cathedral stands near the Esplanade. The present building, erected by convict labour, on a site consecrated in 1838, where old St. Andrew's Church stood from 1837 to 1856, was opened in 1862, and constituted the Cathedral Church of the diocese in 1870. The diocese includes Singapore, Sarawak and Labuan. The Cathedral is an imposing Gothic building surmounted by a fine spire; its length, including the chancel, is 181 feet, the height of the nave is 74 feet and of the spire 207½ feet. The main-door is under the spire at the western end of the Church, and over it is a stained-glass window representing the four evangelists. Close to the main-door stands a marble font of simple and chaste design. A few mural tablets and memorial brasses adorn the walls of the Church. The chancel is lighted by four stained-glass windows covered with floral designs. A fine peal of bells was presented by the heirs of the late Captain J. S. H. Fraser, H.E.I.C.S., in 1889. In the Cathedral compound, which is tastefully laid out

Photo by G. R. Lambert & Co.

ST. ANDREW'S CATHEDRAL AND RAFFLES MONUMENT.

as a garden and adorned with trees and shrubs, stands a monument to Colonel Ronald Macpherson, R.A. (see p. 59), who designed the building.

Hours of Service on Sundays :—7 a.m., 7-45 a.m., and 5-30 p.m. Daily Service at 10 a.m., and 4 p.m.

Sittings in the Cathedral are free at the early morning service, and at all other services after the entrance of the Clergy. The Cathedral is open daily from 7 a.m. to 5-30 p.m.

St. Matthew's Church is an unpretentious building near the General Hospital. Services are held there on Sunday evenings.

St. Andrew's Mission Chapel, on the slope of Fort Canning Hill, near the junction of Stamford Road and Orchard Road. Services are conducted here in English, Malay, Tamil and Chinese. There is a small Mission Chapel also at Jurong.

The Church of England is the Established Church of the Colony; a sum of $18,000 per annum is paid out of the Colonial revenues towards its support.*

2. THE PRESBYTERIAN CHURCH OF ENGLAND.

The Presbyterian Church (commonly called "the Scotch Church") is in Orchard Road, opposite the Ladies' Lawn Tennis Club. The congregation was organised in 1859, and the present Church, a plain building with a decorated porch and belfry, was opened in 1878. It is under the ecclesiastical jurisdiction of the Presbytery of London (North). Hours of Service on Sunday:—7-30 a.m. and 5-30 p.m. Weekly Service:—Wednesdays at 5-15 p.m.

---

* This sum includes the grants for Penang and Malacca, as well as for Singapore.

Services after the Presbyterian form are conducted also in the Reading Rooms of Boustead Institute at 8-15 p.m. and at Keppel Harbour at 9-30 a.m. on Sundays.

There is also a Hokkien Chinese Church in Tanjong Pagar Road, which is supported by and supplies the spiritual needs of a large number of Baba Chinese (Chinese born in the Straits).

Baba Mission Chapel, Prinsep Street. This is the head-quarters of the English Presbyterian Mission to the Chinese, which has stations at Bukit Timah, Saranggong, &c., on the island, and also at Johore Bahru and Muar in the Peninsula.

3. THE METHODIST EPISCOPAL CHURCH.

This is a small Church, in connection with the Methodist Episcopal Mission (American), built about 1897. The Mission has a large and flourishing school attached—the Anglo-Chinese School. Both Church and School are in Coleman Street, at the foot of Fort Canning Hill. Hours of Service on Sunday, in the Church, 9 a.m., 5 p.m. and 8 p.m. Week-night service on Tuesday, at 5-15 p.m.

4. ROMAN CATHOLIC.

The majority of the Christian population of Singapore profess the Roman Catholic faith. The Bishopric of the Diocese of Malacca, which dates from the missionary journey of St. Francis Xavier in the 16th century, is at present held by the Right Rev. Monsignor Barillon. The Cathedral Church of the Good Shepherd is in Bras Basah Road. The foundation-stone was laid in 1843, and the Church opened for Divine Service in 1847. The building is cruciform, surmounted by a spire 161 feet high. Over the high altar stands an image of the Good Shepherd, with a lamb on his shoulder, and on either side, in separate niches, images of SS. Peter and Paul. In the eastern transept is an altar to the Blessed Virgin Mary, on the left of which is a piece of statuary representing Our Lady of Sorrows, holding the dead Christ in her arms. A statue of St. Francis Xavier in his pontifical robes is on the other side. An altar to St. Joseph, with the statue of the Sacred Heart on the left, is in the western transept. The walls of the Church are adorned by fourteen paintings representing scenes from Our Lord's Passion. Over the door in the eastern transept is a large painting of the martyrdom of St. Sebastian. The Church is seated for 700 persons.

There are also the Church of SS. Peter and Paul, Queen Street, and the Church of Our Lady of Lourdes, Ophir Road, the latter being used by the Tamil Mission.

There are two Mission Chapels—St. Joseph's Church at Bukit Timah, and St. Mary's Church at Saranggong. All the foregoing are supported by the French Mission, the Society for the Propagation of the Faith (Paris).

The Procure des Missions Etrangères is at the junction of River Valley Road and Oxley Road.

The Portuguese Catholics own the jurisdiction of the Bishop of Macao, and worship in the Church of St. Joseph, Victoria Street, which is seated for about 500 persons but is now being replaced by one to seat 1000.

5. ARMENIAN.

The Church of St. Gregory, Hill Street, is similar in general external appearance to the Church of the Good Shepherd, and is the oldest ecclesiastical building in Singapore. It was erected in 1835. Hours of Service on Sunday—8.30 to 10 a.m. Daily Services at 6 a.m. and 5 p.m.

6. MISCELLANEOUS.

The Chinese Gospel House, North Bridge Road.

Bethesda Free Meeting House, Bras Basah Road.

The Christian Institute, Waterloo Street.

The Military Chapel at Tanglin is used by different denominations at different hours.

The Y.M.C.A. building is between the Library and the Scotch Church.

JEWISH.

There is a Jewish Synagogue in Waterloo Street, and another at Oxley Rise.

MAHOMMEDAN.

There are a large number of mosques in the island of Singapore. The two best known in town are those in North Bridge Road (Kampong Glam district) and in South Bridge Road, between Tanjong Pagar and the centre of the town. The Malays are all Mahommedan; they were converted to Islam by Arab influences about the 12th or 13th century of the Christian era. Most of the Indians in Singapore profess the Mussulman faith.

INDIAN AND CHINESE TEMPLES.

These are very numerous, and scattered about the town and island everywhere; the most numerous being, of course, the Chinese. They are easily distinguished by their architecture from the mosques, which are severely plain in structure, and from one another; the peculiarities of Indian and Chinese architecture need no description to enable the visitor to distinguish them. The best known of the Indian temples are the so called "Chetty temple"* in Tank Road, and the large temple in South Bridge Road, near the mosque alluded to in the above paragraph.

***

HOSPITALS, &c.

The Government Medical Department is under the Principal Civil Medical Officer, who has control over the following:—

The Quarantine Station at St. John's Island, to the south-west of the harbour, where several thousand coolies can be accommodated at a time awaiting pratique, on their arrival from infected ports.

The General Hospital, situated at Sepoy Lines, about two miles from town. This is a finely situated building, the European Wards of two stories accommodating about 160 beds. In the main building are the administrative offices. A well-found female ward is on the right of the main entrance, and behind this are the native wards, capable of accommodating 300 patients. There were treated at the General Hospital, in 1905, 585 patients in the European wards, and 2,577 in the native wards.

---

* So called, because the Indian Chetties (*i.e.*, money lenders), worship there. Each caste of Indians has a temple of its own; and it seems that there is a temple for every trade or occupation in the town.

The Lunatic Asylum, situated on high ground at the back of the General Hospital, which has an average number of 287 inmates.

The Tan Tock Seng Hospital, in the Saranggong Road about two miles from Town, is the largest hospital in the Colony, with a capacity of 600 beds. This hospital was founded in 1844 by Tan Tock Seng, a wealthy Chinese gentleman; added to in 1884 by his son Tan Kim Cheng; and by public subscription, in 1887. The hospital is now largely supported by the Government, with some subscriptions from Chinese and income from investments, and is under the control of a Committee of Management.

The Maternity Hospital in Victoria Street nearly opposite the Catholic Convent.

The Quarantine Hospital in Balestier Road for cases of infectious and contagious diseases.

The Lock Hospital, in the Bukit Timah Road.

The Prison Hospital, attached to the Civil and Criminal Prisons at Sepoy Lines.

The Straits Medical School, an institution having its quarters in the large building near the entrance to the Prison, founded in 1904 for the training of medical students. The Chinese contributed liberally to the foundation fund of this School.

The total number of patients treated in the hospitals of Singapore in 1905 was 13,015, the total expenditure being $135,804, exclusive of medicines from the Crown Agents.

Originally the General Hospital was in Bukit Timah Road, the building being afterwards used as a Lunatic Asylum, and subsequently as the infectious diseases hospital.

CHAPTER VII.

THE POPULATION OF SINGAPORE.

IN 1819, when Sir Stamford Raffles landed, the population of the island was estimated as under 200. The foundation of a British trading settlement attracted many immigrants both from China and the Archipelago, so that by 1822, the number of inhabitants was reckoned at 10,000. From that time the population has steadily risen till, according to the last census (1901), the grand total of 228,555 has been reached.* The population is very mixed; few nations and languages are unrepresented. The details of the last census are as follows:—Europeans and Americans (including British Military, 495) 3,824; Eurasians, 4,120; Chinese, 164,041; Malays and other natives of the Archipelago,† 36,080; Natives of India and Burmah, 17,823; other nationalities (Arabs, Armenians, Persians, Singhalese, Siamese, Anamese, Japanese, Jews and Negroes), 2,667. It will thus be seen that the Chinese number nearly 72 per cent. of the whole population; but of the 164,041, 15,498 are Straits born (*Babas*). About a third of the Chinese are Hok-kiens (59,117).

The *lingua franca* of the Straits Settlements is Malay (*see* Chap. XV.); which is the language generally used in commerce, and between Asiatics of

---

* In 1826, the population was estimated at 13,732; in 1831, at 20,000; and 1840, at 39,681; in 1881 at 139,208; and in 1891, 184,554.

† These include Achinese, Boyanese, Bugis, Dyaks, Javanese, Jawi Pekkans, and Manilamen. (*See* p. 80.)

different races. It is not uncommon to hear two Chinamen, who speak different dialects of Chinese, conversing in Malay.

The Malays, though not the aborigines of the Peninsula, were the dominant race when the Europeans first came on the scene. Mr. Alfred Russel Wallace thus describes the physical, mental and moral characteristies of this interesting people. "The colour......is a light reddish brown, with more or less of an olive tinge, not varying in any important degree over an extent of country as large as all Southern Europe. The hair is equally constant, being invariably black and straight, and of a rather coarse texture, so that any lighter tint, or any wave or curl in it, is almost certain proof of the admixture of some foreign blood. The face is nearly destitute of beard, and the breast and limbs are free from hair. The stature is tolerably equal, and is always considerably below that of the average European; the body is robust, the breast well-developed, the feet small, thick and short, the hands small and rather delicate, the face is a little broad, and inclined to be flat; the forehead is rather rounded, the brows low, the eyes black and very slightly oblique; the nose is rather small, not prominent, but straight and well-shaped. the apex a little rounded, the nostrils broad and slightly exposed; the cheek-bones are rather prominent, the mouth large, the lips broad and well-cut, but not protruding, the chin round and well-formed.

"In this description there seems little to object to on the score of beauty, and yet, on the whole, the Malays are certainly not handsome. In youth, however, they are often very good-looking, and many of the boys and girls up to twelve or fifteen years of age are very pleasing, and some have countenances which are in their way almost perfect.".................. "In character the Malay is impassive. He exhibits a reserve, diffidence and even bashfulness, which is in some degree attractive, and leads the observer to think that the ferocious and blood-thirsty character imputed to the race must be grossly exaggerated. He is not demonstrative. His feelings of surprise, admiration, or fear are never openly manifested, and are probably not strongly felt. He is slow and deliberate in speech, and circuitous in introducing the subject he has come expressly to discuss.* These are the main features of his moral nature, and exhibit themselves in every action of his life.

"The higher classes of the Malays are exceedingly polite, and have all the quiet ease and dignity of the best-bred Europeans. Yet this is compatible with a reckless cruelty and contempt of human life, which is the dark side of their character.† It is not to be wondered at, therefore, that different persons give totally opposite accounts of them—one praising them for their soberness, civility, and good nature; another abusing them for their deceit, treachery and cruelty."....................."The intellect of the Malay race seems rather deficient. They are incapable of anything beyond the simplest combinations of ideas, and have little taste or energy for the acquirement of knowledge.‡ Their civilization, such as it is, does not seem to be indigenous, as it is entirely confined

---

* This last is a characteristic of most Asiatics.

† It need hardly be said that where British influence is supreme these qualities are repressed, and will probably die out from want of exercise.

‡ This is probably one reason why the Malay literature is imitative rather than original. (*See* Chap. XV.)

to those nations who have been converted to the Mahommedan or Brahminical religions."

Nothing need be added to this description by Mr. Wallace, except that of all the Asiatics in the Straits the Malays are said to be at once the most courtly and the laziest. The religion of the Malays in the Straits Settlements and in the Peninsula is Mahommedan. The Brahminical Malays, referred to above, are found in the islands of Bali and Lombok to the south-east of Java, and also in the hill-country of Java.

In Singapore there are representatives of at least seven Ultra-Peninsular Malay tribes—Achinese, from the north-west of Sumatra; Boyanese, from Bawean, a small island north of Java; Bugis, from the Celebes; Dyaks, the savage tribe of Borneo; Javanese; Jawi Pekkans, or Jawi Perânakkans, a mixed native race, belonging to the Settlement,* and Manilamen from the Philippines. The Malays in Singapore are largely employed in fishing: many take service as coachmen, grooms, gardeners and police. The "boys" in some of the clubs are Malays, and many of the race work as peons or messengers. The younger generation is beginning to take up clerical and other work. The fishing population live in attap houses built on piles on the sea shore between the high and low water mark; and those for whom dwellings are not provided in connection with their work, live in similar houses built inland.

Chinese characteristics are too well-known to need description here. In Singapore they form by

* Born in Singapore, not necessarily Malays. Mothers frequently Malay.

far the largest part of the industrial population, they supply the labour on the plantations, at the docks and wharves; they are bricklayers, carpenters, iron-workers, fitters, engine drivers, boatmen, rikisha coolies, market-gardeners, tailors, shoe-makers, bakers, &c., &c. There are thousands of Chinese shops throughout the town, large and small, stored with goods from all parts of the world. Almost all the domestic servants are Chinese; so are many of the clerks employed in the banks, offices, and stores: and there is a considerable number of prosperous and wealthy Chinese merchants who can hold their own with the European firms. Of the different Chinese races there are representatives of at least five in Singapore—Hok-kiens (the most numerous); Hylams, Cantonese or Macaos (these two, especially the former, are mostly domestic servants); Teo Chews and Kehs.* The peculiarities of Chinese architecture and house decoration may be seen in all parts of the town.

The various Indian races are very variously employed from the Chetty, or money-lender, to the hack-gharry syce, the dhobi (or washerman) and the coolie. Many Indians are employed as messengers in the offices and shops and are shop-keepers themselves; some enter domestic service; while others pursue various industries. The Armenians, Parsees, Arabs and Jews are mainly traders.

The diversity of races, pursuits, languages, customs and dress in Singapore is a source of never failing interest to the observer. The variety of the world and most of its colour is compressed into a few streets before his eyes.

---

* The Hok-kiens come from Amoy, the Teo Chews from the Swatow district, and the Kehs from the Hakka country: while the Hylams come from the island of Hainan.

CHAPTER VIII.

THE SOCIAL LIFE OF SINGAPORE

Very few places have so many Social Clubs and Institutions as Singapore compared with its European population. There are also a large number of Native Clubs and Associations for various objects.

Of the Clubs for indoor recreative and social purposes there are:—

Singapore Club ...	Next to the Post Office.
Masonic Club ...	Coleman Street.
Singapore Catholic Club	Bras Basah Road.
Y. M. C. A. ...	Orchard Road.
Tanglin Club ...	Steven's Road.
Teutonia Club ...	Scott's Road.
Engineers' Association	Battery Road.

Sporting and Athletic Clubs are very numerous, and many of them have handsome pavilions and extensive grounds. The chief are:—

Sporting Club, with Race Course, large paddocks and stands, in Kampong Java Road. Race Meetings are held in May and October each year, and occasionally Gymkhanas. The Polo Club and the Singapore Golf Club also play on the Race Course.

Singapore Cricket Club—Esplanade, for cricket, tennis, football, hockey and lawn bowls.

Singapore Recreation Club—the east end of the Esplanade.

Swimming Club—with a large club-house at Tanjong Rhu.

Straits Chinese Recreation Club—Hong Lim Green.

Rowing Club—Club-house on the river bank near the Public Offices.

There also flourish the Sepoy Lines Golf Club (near General Hospital); the Garrison Golf Club (Tanglin Barracks); Keppel Harbour Golf Club (beyond Keppel Harbour); Ladies' Lawn Tennis Club (Dhoby Ghaut, opposite the Museum); The Singapore Rifle Association (Balestier Road); and Swiss Rifle Club (Bukit Tinggi, five miles out on the Bukit Timah Road).

Of the Literary and Scientific Societies the principal are:—Anglo-Chinese Literary Association; German Reading Club; Royal Asiatic Society (Straits Branch); Straits Medical Association; Straits Philosophical Society; Young Men's Association of the Presbyterian Church.

Musical Societies are the Singapore Philharmonic Society; the Philharmonic Society of St. Cecilia; the Liedertafel.

Singapore is a stronghold of Freemasonry, there being four Lodges; two Royal Arch Chapters; a Mark Lodge; and other bodies. It is the headquarters of the District Grand Lodge of the Eastern Archipelago; and is also a District Grand Chapter. The Board of Benevolence administers the Charity of the Brethren.

The Navy League has a branch here; and there is a Singapore Branch of the Straits Settlements Association.

Numerous Charitable and Religious Societies exist, among them:—British and Foreign Bible

Society; Chinese Christian Association; Confraternity of the Blessed Lady of Rosary and St. Francis Xavier; Children's Aid Society; Destitute Strangers Aid Fund; Society of St. Anthony of Padua; Society of St. Vincent de Paul; Epworth League No. 2360; Women's Christian Temperance Union; Church Work Association; Society for the Protection of Chinese Women and Girls (Poh Leung Kuk), &c., &c.

***

BANKS:—

Banque de l'Indo-Chine, Raffles Place.

Chartered Bank of India, Australia and China,* Battery Road.

Deutsche Asiatische Bank, corner of De Souza and Prince Streets.

Hongkong and Shanghai Banking Corporation, Collyer Quay, opposite Exchange.

International Banking Corporation, corner of Collyer Quay and Prince Street.

Mercantile Bank of India, Limited, 21, Raffles Place.

Nederlandsch Indische Handles-Bank (Netherlands India Commercial Bank), 193, Cecil Street.

Nederlandsche Handel-Maatschappij (Netherlands Trading Society), corner of Cecil and D'Almeida Streets.

ONSULATES:—

American (United States) ...	... Raffles Hotel Buildings, Bras Basah Road.
Austria-Hungary	... 2, D'Souza Street.
Belgium ...	... 3-A, Malacca Street.

* "Chartered Bank," "Mercantile Bank," "Hongkong Bank," are the names to be used in directing native syces.

China ...	... 76, Bras Basah Road.
Denmark ...	... 6 & 7, Telegraph Street.
France ...	... 71-E, River Valley Road.
Germany ...	... 2, D'Souza Street.
Italy ...	... 14, Raffles Quay.
Japan ...	... 97, Robinson Road.
Netherlands ...	... 6, Raffles Quay.
Norway ...	... 18, Collyer Quay.
Portugal ...	... 14, Raffles Quay.
Russia ...	... 71-E, River Valley Road.
Siam ...	... 11, Collyer Quay.
Spain ...	... 71-E, River Valley Road.
Turkey ...	... 2, D'Souza Street.

PRINCIPAL HOTELS:—

Adelphi Hotel	... 1 & 2, Coleman Street.
Caledonian Hotel	... 77, Bras Basah Road.
Grove Hotel ...	... Tanjong Katong.
Hotel Bellevue	... Spottiswoode Park.
Hotel de la Paix	... Coleman Street.
Hotel de l'Europe	... Esplanade.
Hotel Van Wijk	... Stamford Road.
Raffles Hotel ...	... Beach Road.
Recreation Hotel	... Tramway Terminus, Seranggong Road
Sea View Hotel	... Tanjong Katong.
Waverley Hotel	... 59, Hill Street.

POST OFFICE:—*See* p. 61.

TELEGRAPH OFFICE, 3, Raffles Quay.

TELEPHONE CO.'S OFFICES, Hill Street.

NEWSPAPER OFFICES:—

"Singapore Free Press"	29-3, Raffles Place.
"Straits Times"	... Cecil Street.
"Eastern Daily Mail" ...	95, Robinson Road

CHAPTER IX.

SINGAPORE ELECTRIC TRAMWAY.

THE Singapore Electric Tramway Company commenced running on the section from Raffles Hotel to Seranggong in July, 1905. Other sections are (1) from Keppel Harbour, past Tanjong Pagar to Johnston's Pier, and eventually across the River, up High Street, to the Railway Station and on to Orchard Road; (2) Tanjong Pagar through town to Rochore and Gaylang. The Power Station is in McKenzie Road, and not only supplies the tramways but also the Municipal Commissioners with power and lighting. The Municipal distributing station is near St. Andrew's Cathedral. Only a central section of the Town is to have electric lighting, the remainder of the town being lit with gas from the Municipal Gas Works, but the Tramway Company are negotiating for private lighting in the suburb of Tanglin.

Cars are of one class only, the fare is three cents a section. The destination of each car is shown on the front. They stop to pick up passengers wherever required.

SINGAPORE-KRANJI RAILWAY.

This Government Railway runs from the neighbourhood of Keppel (the western) harbour; along the northern shore of the arm of the sea separating Singapore Island from Blakan Mati and Pulau

Brani; at Tanjong Pagar it diverges to the north and runs near the General Hospital to the foot of Fort Canning, crossing Singapore River at Pulau Saigon. Tank Road is the main town station and was till 1906 the southern terminus. The line then runs through Oxley Hill, crosses Orchard Road by an overhead bridge, and debouches on Bukit Timah Road at Newton Station. Thence the track runs alongside the brook and Bukit Timah Road past Cluny and Holland Road (the station for the Swiss Rifle Club) to Bukit Timah. Skirting the southern spurs of the chief eminence of the Island, Bukit Panjang is reached, whence the railway runs down the slope to Woodlands, on the shore of the Straits of Johore—the old Straits, through which, in pre-steam days, all the traffic from the Straits of Malacca to the China Sea passed. A steam ferry conveys the passenger to Johore Town, the capital of the independent State of Johore, a pretty little town, with an excellent State Hotel where the passenger can stay for a short or a long time. There is perhaps not much to see in Johore Town, except the Sultan's Palace or Istana (for which permission must be obtained) and the native quarters of the Town, curious and less European than perhaps any place on the Peninsula. As the mainland terminus of the Peninsular Railway, which is expected to be completed in a few years, Johore may be expected to develop considerably, as the line hence to Malacca, Negri Sembilan, Selangor, Perak and Penang will not only open up much country to agriculture, but will remove Johore from the comparative isolation caused by the dense jungle country lying to the north and round Mount Ophir. The following are the stations on the Singapore-Kranji Railway:—Passir Panjang, Borneo Wharf, Singapore (Tank Road, town terminus), Newton, Cluny Road, Holland Road, Bukit Timah, Bukit Panjang, Woodlands (14 miles from Singapore town terminus). The time table is easily obtainable.

RATES OF HIRE FOR PRIVATE AND HACKNEY CARRIAGES, WITH TABLES OF DISTANCES.

Private Carriages may be hired from the following Livery Stables:—

Abrams' Horse Repository—(H. Abrams), Orchard Road (opposite Government House Gates).

Dallan's Australian Horse Repository, Koek Road, off Orchard Road.

The charge for a carriage and pair is $15 per day or $10 a drive; for a carriage with one horse $10 per day or $5 a time; there being an extra charge, in both cases, if the carriage is used after 7 p.m.

For more than one day the charges are as follows:—

	Carriage and pair.		Carriage and one horse.
One month or more, per day	$5.00	...	$2.50
Half month, per day ...	6.00	...	3.00
One week (7 days), per day	7.00	...	4.00

Saddle horses can be hired at $3.

[N.B.—These charges are approximate.]

Hackney Carriages may be hired at the following rates (2nd class carriages):—

FARES BY DISTANCE.	1 or 2 Persons.	3 or 4 Persons.
For every ½ mile or part thereof	10 cts.	15 cts.

Fares are payable according to *Distance*, unless at the commencement of hiring, the hirer expresses his intention of *paying by time.*

FARES BY TIME.	1 or 2 Persons.	3 or 4 Persons.
	$ *cts.*	$ *cts.*
For every hour or part thereof...	... 60	... 75
For half a day or 5 hours ...	1 50	2 20
For a whole day consisting of nine hours	2 50	3 ...
For every hour or part of an hour after the 5th or 9th hour	... 30	... 40

Detention.—The hirer shall be entitled to detain the carriage for stopping at any place but for every half hour or part of half-an-hour during which any carriage may be detained beyond the first half hour *an additional sum of ten cents* shall be chargeable; and where the fare computed by distance does not amount to 20 cents all detention shall be paid for at the rate of 10 cents *for every half hour or part of half hour.*

Two children under 10 years of age to be counted as one adult person.

Luggage.—For every package carried outside, 10 cents extra for the whole journey, in addition to the fare.

Pace.—Every driver is required to drive at a reasonable and proper speed, not less than 5 miles an hour, unless ordered to drive at a slower pace.

Distance.—No driver shall be required to drive one pony a greater distance than 10 miles in any one day or remain engaged for more than 9 hours at a time.

Drivers are entitled to reckon their fares and claim payment from the place of engagement.

Fares are payable on demand on completion of the engagement.

The owner of every carriage is required to keep a Table of Fares, in legible condition, in the inside of the carriage *under a penalty not exceeding* $10.

Every driver who shall demand or take more than the proper fare is liable to *a penalty not exceeding* $10 for each offence.

JINRIKISHA FARES.

Within Municipal Limits.

BY DISTANCE—

	1st Class.	2nd Class.
For any half mile or fraction of half mile	5 cents.	3 cents.

BY TIME—

For one hour	40 cents.	20 cents.
For every additional quarter of an hour	10 cents.	5 cents.

Detention.—The hirer shall be entitled to detain the Jinrikisha for ten minutes for stopping at any place but for every hour or part of an hour during which any Jinrikisha may be so detained beyond the first ten minutes an additional sum shall be chargeable, viz:—1st class 10 cents, 2nd class 5 cents.

No puller shall be entitled to claim as payment for any distance drawn or any time during which he may be detained in one day more than: 1st class $1.50, 2nd class 80 cents.

All complaints shall be addressed to the Registrar of Jinrikishas, Middle road.

TABLE OF DISTANCES.

From RAFFLES PLACE to	Miles.
Botanical Gardens	$3\frac{1}{2}$
Barracks, Officers' Quarters	$3\frac{1}{4}$
Do. Canteen	4
Bididari Cemetery, Upper Seranggong Road	$4\frac{1}{4}$
Cemetery, Bukit Timah Road	$2\frac{1}{4}$
Central Police Station	$\frac{1}{2}$
Clyde Terrace Market	$1\frac{1}{4}$
Criminal Prison	$1\frac{1}{2}$
Cross Roads, Tanglin...	3
Ellenborough Market...	$\frac{3}{4}$
Cathedral of the Good Shepherd	1
Tanglin and Teutonia Clubs	$2\frac{3}{4}$

	Miles.
General Hospital	$1\frac{1}{2}$
Government House	2
Hackney Carriage Registration Office, Middle Road ...	$1\frac{1}{2}$
Head Quarters Office, Pearls' Hill	1
Hotel de l'Europe, Cricket Pavilion, Supreme Court, and Town Hall	$\frac{1}{2}$
Johnston's Pier, Singapore Club, Post Office and Shipping Office	$\frac{1}{4}$
Kandang Kerbau Police Station	$1\frac{3}{4}$
Ladies' Lawn Tennis Ground, Raffles Museum and Presbyterian Church...	$1\frac{1}{4}$
Lunatic Asylum	2
Masonic Hall and Methodist Church	$\frac{3}{4}$
Municipal Store, River Valley Road	1
Municipal Offices	$\frac{1}{2}$
Newton Railway Station, Bukit Timah Road	$2\frac{3}{4}$
Orchard Road Market	$1\frac{3}{4}$
Do. Police Station	$2\frac{1}{2}$
Pauper Hospital	$2\frac{3}{4}$
Race Course, Grand Stand and Golf Club	$2\frac{1}{2}$
Rochore Market and Police Station	2
St. Andrew's Cathedral, Sailors' Home, Adelphi Hotel and Hotel de la Paix...	$\frac{3}{4}$
Raffles Hotel and School	$\frac{3}{4}$
Railway Station, River Valley Road	1
Slaughter House, Kampong Saigon	$1\frac{1}{4}$
Tyersall (H. H. Sultan of Johore)	$4\frac{1}{4}$
Water Works, Thomson Road	5
Wayang Satu Police Station	$3\frac{3}{4}$
Tanjong Pagar Wharf	$1\frac{1}{2}$
Do. (west end) French and German Mails, Landing Pier from Blakang Mati	$2\frac{1}{4}$
P. & O. Company's Wharf	$2\frac{3}{4}$
Keppel Harbour Dock	$3\frac{1}{2}$

In making the above computations fractions under 2 furlongs have been reckoned as $\frac{1}{4}$ mile.

The Government mile stones are measured from the centre gate of Police Bahru, opposite St. Andrew's Cathedral.

Visitors to Singapore are warned against the extortionate charges made by the gharry-syces. The above tables give the legal fares. When a dispute arises, the order to drive to the Police Station (*Pergi ka rumah pasong*) will bring the syce to reason, if his charges are exorbitant. Another trick of gharry-syces is to drive to their destination by a circuitous route, so as to be able to demand legally more than their proper fare.*

A few of the native syces know the English names of places, but the majority do not. A list of the names of the principal buildings and places of interest, in Malay, is therefore appended, to aid visitors in finding their way about the town and island. Syces generally know Hotels by their names.

Borneo Wharf ...	(English Name)
Botanical Gardens ...	*Kebun Bungah.*
Bukit Timah ...	*Bukit Timah.*
Cathedral Church of the Good Shepherd ...	*Greja Franchis.*
Cemetery (Christian) ...	*Kuboran Orang Puteh.*
Chartered Bank of India, Australia and China ...	Chartered Bank.
Mercantile Bank of India, Ltd.	Mercantile Bank.
Chinese Protectorate ...	*Pikring punya Ofis.*
Convent ...	*Skola Franchis Perampuan.*
Criminal Prison ...	Goal.
Explanade ...	*Padang Besar*
Fort Canning ...	*Bukit Bandera.*
Gas Works ...	*Tempat Api Gas.*
General Hospital ...	Hospital or *Rumah Orang Sakit, Sepoy Lines.*
German Club ...	*Kongsee Orang Jerman.*

* When asked the amount of their fare syces generally answer *Tuan* (or *Mem*) *punya suka*, *i.e.*, " what Master (or Madam) pleases." No more than the legal fare should be given.

Government House	... *Gebenor punya Rumah.*
Government Offices	... *Second Gebenor punya Ofis.*
Hongkong & Shanghai Banking Corporation	... Hongkong Bank.
Impounding Reservoir	... *Kolam Ayer Besar.*
Johnston's Pier	... (English Name)
Ladies Lawn Tennis Club	... *Club Perampuan.*
Livery Stables	... *Tuan——* punya Tempat Kuda.*
Lunatic Asylum	... *Rumah Orang Gila.*
Police Courts	... *Polis.*
Market	... *Pasar.*
Master Attendant's Office	... *Shahbander punya Ofis* or *Ofis Khlasi.*
Masonic Hall	... *Rumah Hantu.*
Maternity Hospital	... *Kompani punya Tempat Obat.*
Methodist Episcopal Church.	*Greja dekat Rumah Hantu.*
Mount Faber	... *Bukit Bandera, Teluk Blangah.*
Municipal Offices	... *Ofis Chukei Pintu.*
Keppel Harbour Dock	... (English Name) or *Pulau Hantu.*
Orchard Road	... *Jalan Besar.*
Pauper Hospital	... *Rumah Miskin.*
Pearls' Hill (Head Quarters' Office)	... *Bukit Komshariat.*
P. & O. Wharf	... (English Name) or *Teluk Blangah.*
Police Station	... *Rumah Pasong.*
Police Station (Central)	... *Rumah Pasong Besar, Polis Lama.*
Post Office	... (English Name)
Presbyterian Church	... *Greja Kechil.*
Race Course	... *Tempat Lumbak Kuda.*
Railway Station	... *Station Kreta Api.*
Raffles Girls' School	... *Skola Missy.*
Raffles Institution (Boys' School)	... *Skola Besar.*
Raffles Library and Museum.	*Rumah Gambar.*
Reservoir (High Level)	... *Kolam Ayer.*
Rifle Range (Balestier)	... *Tembak Saser.*
St. Andrew's Cathedral	... *Greja Besar.*
St. Andrew's Mission Chapel.	*Greju Besar punya Mission.*

* Here insert the name of the proprietor.

St. Gregory's Church (Armenian)	... *Orang Armenis punya Greja.*
St. Joseph's Institution ("Brothers' School")	... *Skola Franchis Jantan.*
Sailors' Home	... *Rumah Khlasi.*
Sepoy Lines	... (English Name)
Singapore Club	... Do.
Supreme Court	... *Court Besar.*
Tanglin	... *Tanglin.*
Tanjong Pagar	... *Tanjong Pagar.*
Telegraph Office	... *Telegrap.*

NOTE:—The Malay vowels are pronounced as in Italian (*a*=*ah*; *e*=*ay*; *i*=*ee*; o=*oh*; *u*=*oo*; *ou*=*ow*). With regard to consonants *g* is always hard; *j* and *ch* are pronounced as in English. Final *ng* has a slightly nasal sound; *s* is pronounced strongly, but never like the English *z*. Final *k* is not sounded. The word *kechil* (=" little ") is pronounced *kitchy* in Singapore.

The following words and phrases may be found useful:—

Drive to——	... *Pergi* ka——*
Go on. Drive on	... *Jalan.*
Stop	... *Berhenti*†
Turn (Turn the Carriage)	... *Pusing (Pusing kreta).*
Harness the Horse	... *Pakei Kuda.*
Unharness the Horse	... *Buka Kuda.*
Get ready the Carriage	... *Pasang Kreta.*‡
Light the Lamps	... *Pasang Pelita* (or *Lampo).*
What is your fare?	... *Berapa Sewa?*
Too much	... *Banyak chukup.*
Drive to A. B. & Co.	... *Pergi ka A. B. & Co. punya Gedong (or Godown).*
Come back here in an hour	... *Balik ka-sini lagi satu jam.*
Wait a little	... *Nanti sa' buntar* (or *nanti dahulu*‖)
Go fast	... *Jalan lakas.*

* Pronounce *Piggy.*
† Pronounce *Brenti.*
‡ The Portuguese word *Carreta*
‖ Pronounce *Dooloo.*

Go slow	... *Jalan perlahan-perlahan.**
How many miles is it to Selitar?	... *Selitar berapa batu?*
Off with you!	... *Pulang!*
Return to the ship	... *Balik ka kapal.*
Policeman	... *Mata-mata*
Hack-Gharry	... *Kreta Sewa.*
Dollar	. *Ringgit.*
Cent	... *Sen.*
Jinrikisha	... *Kreta Hongkong.*

NUMERALS.

One	... *Satu*
Two	... *Dua*
Three	... *Tiga*
Four	... *Ampat*
Five	... *Lima*
Six	... *Anam*
Seven	... *Tujoh*
Eight	... *Lapan (Dilapan)*
Nine	... *Sembilan*
Ten	... *Sa'puloh*
Eleven	... *Sa'blas*
Twelve, thirteen, &c.	... *Dua blas, tiga blas, &c.*
Twenty	... *Dua puloh*
Twenty-one, &c.	... *Dua puloh satu, &c.*
Thirty	... *Tiga puloh*
Forty, fifty, &c.	... *Ampat puloh, lima puloh, &c.*
Hundred	... *Ratus.*
100, 200, 300, &c.	... *Sa'ratus, dua ratus, tiga ratus, &c.*
795	... *Tujoh ratus sembilan puloh lima.*

Visitors will do well to buy the "Malay Pronouncing Hand-book," published by Fraser & Neave, Limited, which contains most of the phrases in common use; they will find it extremely useful during their stay in port.

---

* Pronounce *Plan-plan.*

CHAPTER X.

Steam Communication between Singapore and other Ports.

The position of Singapore, on the Great Mail Route from Europe to the Far East, is a favourable one for rapid and direct communication with all parts of the world. Its situation amongst the hundreds of islands in the Malay Archipelago makes it an important centre from which a large fleet of local steamers sails in every direction.

The regular mail service to and from Europe is as follows:—

Outwards.—On Saturday mornings, alternately by the Peninsular & Oriental Co.'s steamers via Colombo and by the British India Steam Navigation Co.'s steamers via India. These bring the mail closing in London three weeks previously.

Homewards.—Closing each Thursday afternoon, alternately by the Peninsular & Oriental Co.'s and the British India Steam Navigation Co.'s regular Mail Steamers.

There is also a fortnightly mail service both outwards and homewards by the Messageries Maritimes (French Mail), the Norddeutscher Lloyd (German Mail), and the Stoomvaart Maatschappij Nederland (Dutch Mail).

Besides these the P. & O. Co. run their Intermediate Line outward and homeward (most of them carrying passengers) fortnightly.

Branch mail lines (French and Dutch) run to Batavia weekly; and French (fortnightly) to Saigon. The British India Steam Navigation Co. despatch a weekly steamer to Port Swettenham, Penang, Rangoon and Calcutta; every fortnight to Madras and Coromandel Coast Ports; and one every two months to Australia.

Following is a list of the principal steamship companies and their regular routes:—

P. & O. Co.—Outward mail alternate Saturdays to Hongkong, Shanghai and Japan. Homeward mail alternate Thursdays to Penang, Colombo, connecting with the homeward mail from Australia. Intermediate direct service fortnightly both ways, mostly carrying passengers and calling at Marseilles.

MESSAGERIES MARITIMES DE FRANCE.—Fortnightly to Europe via Colombo, and outwards to Saigon, China and Japan. A branch line fortnightly to Batavia, and one to Saigon after the arrival of the P. & O. mail.

NORDDEUTSCHER LLOYD.—Imperial German mail line fortnightly to and from Bremen/Hamburg to Antwerp, Rotterdam, Southampton, Gibraltar, Genoa, Naples, Port Said, Suez, Aden, Colombo, Penang, Singapore, Hongkong, Shanghai, Nagasaki, Kobe and Yokohama. Connecting lines of N. D. L. steamers sail from Singapore to Siam, Netherlands India, Borneo and the Philippines.

HAMBURG-AMERIKA LINIE.—Fortnightly service between Hamburg, Bremen, Antwerp and Rotterdam and the Straits, China and Japan.

NIPPON YUSEN KAISHA.—Imperial Japanese Mail Service fortnightly to and from Yokohama, Kobe, Hongkong, Singapore, Penang, Colombo, Marseilles, London and Antwerp. Also a service Japan-Bombay via Singapore.

STOOMVAART-MAATSCHAPPIJ "NEDERLAND."—Fortnightly service between Java and Amsterdam, via Singapore, Sabang Bay, Port Said and Genoa.

AUSTRO-HUNGARIAN LLOYDS.—Monthly service to Trieste.

BRITISH INDIA STEAM NAVIGATION CO.—Weekly service to Penang, Rangoon and Calcutta. Fortnightly mail service Singapore, Penang, Negapatam and Madras. To Australia every two months. Weekly to Port Swettenham (Selangor) and Penang.

APCAR LINE.—Hongkong to Calcutta via Singapore, Penang and Rangoon.

ISLAND LINE.—Six weekly service between Sydney and Singapore, via Thursday Island, British New Guinea, New Britain and North Queensland Ports.

STRAITS STEAMSHIP CO.—Daily for ports on the west coast of the Malay Peninsula.

KONINGKLIJKE PAKETVAART MAATSCHAPPIJ.—To and from Netherlands Indies ports, every few days.

EAST ASIATIC CO., LTD.—Weekly service between Singapore and Bangkok, via ports on East Coast of Malay Peninsula.

WEE BIN LINE OF STEAMERS.—To Netherland Indies Ports, also a service to ports on West side of Malay Peninsula.

HEAP ENG MOH LINE OF STEAMERS.—Singapore to Batavia, Cheriton and Samarang.

PRINCIPAL STEAMSHIP LINES, AND AGENTS.

Amiral Line—Moine Comte & Co., Change Alley.

Apcar & Co.'s Calcutta and China Steamers—Paterson, Simons & Co., Prince Street.

Austrian Lloyd's Steam Navigation Co.—Rautenberg, Schmidt & Co., 4, Cecil Street.

British India Steam Navigation Co.—Boustead & Co., Collyer Quay.

Canadian Pacific Steam Ship Co.—Boustead & Co., Collyer Quay.

China Mutual Steam Navigation Co.—W. Mansfield & Co., Ltd., 9, Collyer Quay.

Compagnie des Messageries Maritimes de France—1, Robinson Road.

Currie, A., & Co.'s Indian and Australian Line—McAlister & Co., Ltd., Battery Road.

Deutsche Dampschiff Rhederei zu Hamburg—Rautenberg, Schmidt & Co., 4, Cecil Street.

East Asiatic Co., Ltd.,—6 and 7, Telegraph Street.

Eastern & Australian Steam Ship Co.—Guthrie & Co., Ltd., Collyer Quay.

Glen Line—Boustead & Co., Collyer Quay.

Heap Eng Moh Line of Steamers—Heap Eng Moh, 22, Teluk Ayer Street.

Indo-China Steam Navigation Co.—Boustead & Co., Collyer Quay.

Kingsin Line—Rautenberg, Schmidt & Co., 4, Cecil Street.

Koninklijke Paketvaart Maatschappij—J. Daendels & Co., Ltd., 2 & 3, Collyer Quay.

Navigaziona Generale Italiana—Behn, Meyer & Co., Ltd., De Souza Street and Collyer Quay.

Norddeutscher-Lloyd, Bremen—Behn, Meyer & Co., Ltd., De Souza Street and Collyer Quay

Ocean Steam Ship Co., Ltd.—W. Mansfield & Co., Ltd., 9, Collyer Quay.

PacificMail SteamShipCo.-Adamson,Gilfillan& Co., Ltd.,15,CollyerQuay

Peninsular and Oriental Steam Navigation Co.—Corner of Robinson Road and Japan Street.

Queensland Royal Mail Line—Boustead & Co., Collyer Quay.

Shire Line—Boustead & Co., Collyer Quay.

Stoomvaart Maatschappij "Nederland"—J. Daendels & Co., Ltd., 2, and 3, Collyer Quay.

Straits Steam Ship Co., Ltd.—Raffles Quay.

Transatlantic Co.—Barlow & Co. 5, d'Almeida Street.

Wee Bin Line of Steamers—Wee Bin & Co., 106, Market Street.

West Australian Steam Navigation Co.—Boustead & Co., Collyer Quay

CHAPTER XI.

CURRENCY, WEIGHTS, MEASURES, TIME.

CURRENCY.

THE standard coin of the Straits Settlements and its dependencies, the Federated Malay States, British North Borneo and Johore, is the Straits Settlements dollar. The millesimal fineness is 900, its standard weight 312 grains (20.217 grammes); and its minimum weight as currency 308 grains (19.958 grammes).

The coinage of the Colony consists (besides the dollar) of four silver and three copper pieces; the silver coins being—the half-dollar (50 cents), and pieces of 20, 10, and 5 cents respectively in value. The three copper coins are one-cent, half-cent, and quarter-cent pieces.

Government Currency Notes of the value of $1, $5, $10, $20, $25, $50, $100, and $500 are also issued, against a treasury reserve of dollars and sterling securities. The Chartered Bank of India, Australia and China also issues notes, as did formerly the Hongkong and Shanghai Bank. The Government Note Issue is about 20 million dollars, and the paper is readily accepted all over British Malaya.

The Straits subsidiary silver coinage (20, 10 & 5 cents pieces) is legal tender up to $2; the copper coinage up to $1.

The sterling exchange value of the dollar has varied enormously during the last quarter of a century. From 4*s.* 2*d.* it steadily went down, reaching its lowest point—1*s.* 6$\frac{5}{8}$*d.*—in 1902. It then rose, with various fluctuations, and at the end of 1905 was about 2*s.* 4*d.* In January, 1906, the Government fixed the rate of exchange at 2*s.* 4*d.* to the dollar. The sovereign is now legal tender, and £7 are equal to $60. The Government have the option of redeeming their notes, and receiving and paying in either gold or silver at the rate of 2*s.* 4*d.* to the dollar.

WEIGHTS AND MEASURES.

The weights and Measures used throughout the Colony are:—

Lineal Measure.

12 Inches	... ... = ...	1 Foot.
3 Feet	... ... = ...	1 Yard.
5½ Yards	... ... = ...	1 Pole or Perch.
40 Poles	... ... = ...	1 Furlong.
8 Furlongs	... ... = ...	1 Mile.

The English *mile* is called by the Malays *Batu* (*i.e.*, Stone).

Superficial Measure.

144 Sq. Inches	... = ...	1 Sq. Foot.
9 Sq. Feet ...	... = ...	1 Sq. Yard.
30¼ Sq. Yards...	... = ...	1 Pole.
40 Poles	... ... = ...	1 Rood.
4 Roods	... ... = ...	1 Acre.

Avoirdupois Weight.

16 Drams	... ... = ...	1 Ounce.
16 Ounces	... ... = ...	1 Pound.
14 Pounds	... ... = ...	1 Stone.
8 Stone	... ... = ...	1 Hundredweight.
20 Hundredweight	... = ...	1 Ton.

Measures of Capacity.

Dry Measure.

2 Gills	...	... = ...	1 Pau or Quarter Chupak.
2 Pau	...	... = ...	1 Pint or Half Chupak.
2 Pints	...	... = ...	1 Quart or Chupak.
4 Quarts	...	... = ...	1 Gallon or Gantang.
2 Gallons	...	... = ...	1 Peck.
4 Pecks	...	... = ...	1 Bushel.
8 Bushels	...	... = ...	1 Quarter.

Liquid Measure.

2 Gills	...	... = ...	1 Pau or Quarter Chupak.
2 Pau	...	... = ...	1 Pint or Half Chupak.
2 Pints	...	... = ...	1 Quart or Chupak.
4 Quarts	...	... = ...	1 Gallon or Gantang.
63 Gallons	...	... = ...	1 Hogshead
2 Hogsheads		... = ...	1 Pipe.
2 Pipes	...	... = ...	1 Tun.

The following local customary weights are also in use in the Colony :—

Avoirdupois Weight.

1 Tahil	...	... = ...	($1\frac{1}{3}$ oz. Avoirdupois.)
16 Tahil	...	... = ...	1 Kati ($1\frac{1}{3}$ lb.)
100 Kati	...	... = ...	1 Pikul ($133\frac{1}{3}$ lbs.)
40 Pikul	...	... = ...	1 Koyan ($5,333\frac{1}{3}$ lb.)

Goldsmiths' Weight.

12 Saga	=	1 Mayam	=	52 Grains.
16 Mayam	=	1 Bongkal	=	832 Grains.
12 Bongkal	=	1 Kati	=	9,954 Grains (1 lb. 8 oz. 16 dwt.)

Opium Weight.

10 Tee	...	... = ...	1 Hoon
10 Hoon	...	... = ...	1 Chee
10 Chee	...	... = ...	1 Tahil

The English method of computing time is adopted in Singapore, though the Mahommedans reckon the day of 24 hours from sunset to sunset, and keep to their system of lunar months.

The days of the week are as follows:—

English.	*Colloquial.* *	*Malay.* †
Sunday ...	... Hari Minggo ‡	.. Hari Ahad
Monday ...	... Hari Satu	... Hari Ithnain
Tuesday ...	... Hari Dua	... Hari Thalatha
Wednesday	... Hari Tiga	... Hari Raubu
Thursday	... Hari Ampat	... Hari Khamis
Friday ...	... Hari Lima	... Hari Jemaat §
Saturday ...	... Hari Anam	... Hari Sabtu

The Mean Time of the 105th Meridian is adopted in the Straits Settlements and Federated Malay States, which is therefore seven hours in advance of Greenwich mean time.

There are two time balls erected for the convenience of the shipping, one at Fort Canning and one at Mount Faber, where the time observatory is situated. These balls drop at 1 P.M. local time. Tell-tale clocks giving the hour by signals are also placed on the wharf at Tanjong Pagar and in the Master Attendant's Office.

The mid-day gun at Fort Canning is fired by electricity from the Standard clock.

---

* Used in Singapore commonly.

† The Malays have borrowed the Arabic names for the days of the week—*Yaum-ul-ahad, Yaum-ul-ithnain,* &c.

‡ *Minggo* is a corruption of the Portuguese word *Domingo.*

§ The Mahommedan Sabbath—from 6 p.m. on Thursday to 6 p.m. on Friday.

CHAPTER XII.

Imports, Exports, Shipping, &c., Singapore.

SINGAPORE being not a terminus, but an *entrepôt* of trade, it is to be expected that the imports will exceed the exports to a considerable extent. In former years the receiving of cargo for re-shipment to other ports was one of the chief parts of local commerce; but, though the business done now is still very large, it is slowly but surely contracting, owing to the rapid multiplication of through-steamers, which touch, but do not break bulk here. This fact leads some to believe that the town has seen its best days; but others, looking further ahead, see, in the mineral and other resources of the Malay Peninsula, reason to believe in a great future for the capital of the Straits Settlements. As a coaling station, Singapore must always hold a position of the first importance in the Far East, and the rapid increase of steamships on the Eastern seas will enhance its importance.

The Imports for the year 1905 (excluding Treasure), were valued at $238,347,216 (£24,331,589), and the Exports at $197,618,811 (£20,157,730).

The Straits Settlements Blue Book for 1905, gives the following particulars of Imports and Exports:—

IMPORTS.

From the United Kingdom	$ 26,367,037
„ British Colonies and Protectorates (including British India)	100,935,203
„ Foreign Countries	115,997,985
„ Penang and Malacca	5,681,332
Total ...	$ 248,981,557

EXPORTS.

To the United Kingdom	$	31,623,648
„ British Colonies and Protectorates (including British India)		55,017,209
„ Foreign Countries		117,254,180
„ Penang and Malacca		7,796,869
Total ...	$	211,691,906

The largest imports come from the Dutch Indies, Siam (and its dependencies), Japan and China; the largest exports go to the United Kingdom, Siam (and its dependencies), America, Hongkong, France and India. The chief exports from Singapore of late years have been gambier, tin, sago, pepper, gutta, rattans, tapioca and copra.

From the Blue Book for 1905, are also taken the following particulars as to Shipping at the port of Singapore during that year.

ENTRANCES.

	Number.	Tons.
Merchant Vessels—		
British	2,707	3,862,253
Foreign	2,535	2,500,205
Native Craft—		
British	5,222	346,042
Foreign	4,847	225,783
Warships, &c.—		
British	75	256,254
Foreign	106	220,751
Total ...	15,492	7,411,288

CLEARANCES.

	Number.	Tons.
Merchant Vessels—		
British	2,718 ...	3,883,441
Foreign	2,550 ...	2,518,475
Native Craft—		
British	5,354 ...	358,302
Foreign	4,794 ...	224,233
Warships, &c.—		
British	75 ...	256,254
Foreign	106 ...	220,751
	15,597	7,461,456

CHAPTER XIII.

The Federated Malay States.

NO Guide book to Singapore would be complete without at least some reference to the neighbouring Peninsula and its thriving Native States. Prior to 1876 the land from the latitude of Penang Island consisted of Malay Independent States: Perak, Pahang, Selangor, Sungei Ujong, the Negri Sembilan (nine states—chief among them Rembau, Johol), Malacca (British territory) and Johore (independent). In 1876 the murder of Mr. J. W. W. Birch led to an expedition to Perak, and a British Resident was installed there. Violence in Sungei Ujong in 1880 led to similar action there. In 1882, a British Resident was appointed to Selangor, and ten years later one in Pahang, the east-coast state. In 1895 the states were Federated, and a Resident-General appointed.

Briefly the system of Government is to place the disposal of the revenue under the British Resident and his officers. Religion and native customs are administered by the Sultan and his Council, who also consider proposed legislation. The Sovereign is granted a handsome allowance from the revenues of the state, but, except as regards religion and native customs, the states are administered by the British Residents, subject to the direction of the Resident-General, who resides at Kuala Lumpur, and is himself beneath the rule of the Governor of the Straits Settlements as High Commissioner for the Federated Malay States.

The states and their chief ports and capitals are as follows:—

Negri Sembilan (Port Dickson); capital, Seremban; important places, Kuala Pilah, Gemas.

Selangor (Port Swettenham); capital, Kuala Lumpur (also the federal capital); other places, Klang (coastal), Kuala Kubu, Sungei Besi (mining).

Perak (Port Weld, or by railway from Prai, Province Wellesley, opposite Penang); capital Taiping; important places, Ipoh and Batu Gajah (mining).

Pahang (Kuantan and Pekan, east coast); capital, Kuala Lipis; important places, Raub, Bentong.

The visitor to Singapore with a week or so to spare cannot do better than visit these Native States, which are well-developed by their railways, have large planting interests, and produce two-thirds of the alluvial tin of the world.

The steamers of the Straits Steamship Co. sail (Sundays excepted) daily for the west coast ports. They have good passenger accommodation and there are hotels at Kuala Lumpur, and rest-houses at other important places. A few trips are indicated.

Singapore, Port Swettenham, Kuala Lumpur (one night); rail to Seremban, Port Dickson, catch the boat on return to Singapore (Friday night to Monday morning).

Singapore, Malacca, train to Seremban, Port Dickson and back. Or Seremban to Kuala Lumpur (train and stay one night) return via Port Swettenham.

Singapore, Port Dickson or Port Swettenham, Kuala Lumpur, rail to Kuala Kubu (good rest-house) Tapah, Ipoh, Taiping, or Prai. Ferry to Penang, return by boat. (Five days quickly, or eight leisurely).

The area of the F. M. S. is 26,380 sq. miles. Population about 840,000 (one-third Chinese). Imports $46,955,742 in 1904; exports $77,620,084, of which tin is $60,000,000 (fifty thousand tons.) Rubber is the agricultural industry of the F. M. S. At the end of 1906, there were 13 million trees planted, on 100,000 acres, and 385 tons of rubber were produced, of a value of £200,000.

CHAPTER XIV.

THE FAUNA, FLORA, AND GEOLOGY OF SINGAPORE.

I.—THE FAUNA OF SINGAPORE ISLAND.

(Abridged from notes kindly supplied by WILLIAM DAVISON, ESQ., *late Curator of the Raffles Library and Museum, Singapore.)*

MAMMALIA.—Singapore Island is not rich in in genera, species, or individuals of Mammalia. The ruminants have been almost exterminated within the last few years; and it may be safely asserted that some species of the smaller Carnivora, noted as occurring by Dr. Cantor, are not now found wild on the Island. There are in Singapore 23 genera of mammals, comprising 40 species:—

Quadrumana (monkeys) 2 genera, 3 species, 1.—*Semnopithecus obscurus*,* found in the jungle, but rare; 2.—*Macacus cynomolgus* (*M. carbonarius*), the fishing monkey, common on wooded banks of streams and in mangrove swamps; 3.—*Macacus aureas*, the rusty macaque, in the jungle and plantations.†

The *Bats* have not yet been sufficiently worked out; two fruit-eating, and about 15 insectivorous species are recorded. The best known of the former is the so-called "Flying-Fox" (*Pteropus edulis*); the average adult size being 12 inches long and 4 or 5 feet in expanse.‡ The other is much smaller (*Cynopterus marginatus*). The Colugo or Flying Lemur (*Galeopithecus volans*) occurs, but rarely, in the jungle.

---

* The *Lotong* of the Malays.

† The Pig-tailed monkey (*Macacus nemestrinus*—the *Bruk* of the Malays) is often imported by the natives, and trained to climb coconut palms to gather the nuts. It is common in the Peninsula.

‡ This bat is often to be seen in the early morning in the suburbs.

Two species of tree-shrews are found—*Tupia ferruginea* and *T. javanica*; and one musk-shrew—*Sorex (Crocidura) murina*, which is distributed over the whole oriental region.

Carnivora.—The largest on the island is the tiger (*Felis tigris*); the tigers, much less common than formerly,* are immigrants from the mainland, swimming over the Johore Strait to the island. The dislike of leopards to water, accounts for these animals, common on the mainland, not being found in Singapore.

Two otters † occur—*Lutra barang* and *Aonyx leptonyx*—and one civet (*Viverricula malaccensis*).||

Of squirrels there are two species, and possibly a third. § There are *Sciurus notatus* and *S. griseimanus*. A flying squirrel, *Sciuropterus*, is not uncommon in the jungle.

The rats and mice of the island are not yet systematically worked out. The following are known to occur:—*Mus bandicoota*, the giant-rat or bandicoot (rare), *M. decumanus*, the brown rat, *M. musculus*, the common mouse—all probably introduced species.

The wild pig (*Sus indicus*) was once very plentiful, and is still found in the jungle and plantations.

Ruminantia.—Two species survive—*Rusa equinus*, which has almost disappeared, and *Tragulus Kanchil*, the lesser moose-deer, also rare.

Aquatic Mammalia.—The dugong or sea-cow (*Halicore dugong*) and a dolphin (probably *Delphinus plumbeus*) are found in the neighbouring waters; the latter ascends the larger streams for a considerable distance.

AVES.—The systematic working out of the birds of Singapore will, doubtless, add considerably to the number of species known to occur. At present 219 species are recorded—permanent residents, regular migrants, or mere stragglers.

---

* It is said that between 1860 and 1870, more than 50 persons were killed by tigers.

† Called by the Malays *Anjing ayer*—*i.e.*, water dogs.

|| The *Musang* of the Malays: it haunts the roofs and floors of the houses.

§ Perhaps *Sciurus tenuis*.

Raptores.—Neither diurnal nor nocturnal birds of prey are extensively represented in the island. The commonest are the white-bellied sea-eagle (*Haliœtus leucogaster*) and the maroon-kite (*Haliastur indus*). Less common is the black-legged falconet (*Microhierax fringillarius*). Inhabiting the woods, the Besra sparrow-hawk (*Accipiter virgatus*), the changeable hawk-eagle (*Spizaetus limnaetus*), the serpent-eagle (*Spilornis Rutherfordi*), the Osprey (*Pandion haliaetus*). Hume's honey-buzzard (*Pernis tweeddalii*) has so far been found in Singapore only. Two specimens have been captured, one of which is now in the British Museum. Of the owls the commonest are *Scops lempigi*, *S. malayanus*, *S. rufescens*, and *Ninox scutata*, the Raffles hawk-owl.

Swallows, swifts and swiftlets (*Collocalia* *) are common on the island: the crested tree-swift (*Macropteryx longipennis*) has been known to occur.

The Malay night-jar (*Caprimulgus macrurus*) is very common, and its monotonous cry may be heard from dusk to dawn, especially on moon-light nights. Other night-jars occur, but rarely. There are 5 species of bee-eaters, the commonest being *Merops sumatranus*, *M. philippinus* and *M. swinhoei*. King-fishers abound in all parts of the island; 12 species are recorded—4 of stork-billed king-fishers (*Pelargopsis*), 4 of the family *Halcyon*, 2 of the three-toed king-fishers (*Ceyx*) and 2 small blue ones (*Alcedo*). Four varieties of broad-bill have been collected on the island, but they seem to have disappeared altogether in recent times. †

The long tailed parroquet (*Palœornis longicauda*) occurs occasionally in small flocks, probably as partial migrants from the mainland. The Malayan parrot (*Psittacus incertus*) is occasionally seen, most probably a migrant. The Malayan loriquet (*Loriculus galgulus*) is not uncommon about plantations and other suitable localities.‡ 14 species of woodpeckers are recorded, 6 species of barbets, and 6 species of true cuckoos. To these must be added a few aberrant members of the *Cuculidœ*, not parasitical, but

* These are the birds that build edible nests. The nest of one species, *C. linchi*, is not sufficiently pure to be of any economic value.

† Two species of hornbills (*Buceros rhinoceroides* and *Hydrocissa convexa*), are noted as occurring in the island, the former by Diard, the latter by Wallace. I have not met with them.—*W. D.*

‡ A favourite cage bird with the Malays.

building their own nests and rearing their own young. This family includes the so-called crow-pheasants or coucols, of which four species are known to occur in the island. The sun birds are very numerous, both in species and individuals. Some of them rival in the brilliancy of their plumage the humming-birds of the New World. The flower-peckers are a group of small birds, many of them brilliantly coloured, the plumage having generally a metallic gloss; two species are found in Singapore. Four true shrikes occur; they are all migratory* the most common being the brown shrike *(Lanius cristatus)*† and the thick billed-shrikes *(L. magnirostris)*. Two species of cuckoo-shrikes are recorded; and four species of minivets, which though common on the Peninsula, are rare on the island.

The crow-billed drongo *(Dicrurus annectans)* occurs, and also the beautiful racket-tailed drongo *(Dissemururus paradiseus)* is still not uncommon in the better wooded portions of the island. It has a wonderful variety of notes, and has the power of imitating the notes of other birds and animals. The bronzed drongo *(Chaptia œnea)* is not numerous, but a few occur in the jungle. The allied paradise flycatcher *(Terpsiphone affinis)* is found on the island, but rarely.

The above notes on the birds are necessarily very brief and incomplete, a mere catalogue of the names of the great variety of Singapore birds would occupy more space than is here available.

REPTILIA.—*Snakes.*—The following is a table of the Snakes of Singapore. The non-venomous snakes include all the burrowing, fresh-water, and many of the ground and tree snakes. Though a large number of venomous snakes occur in the island there is no authentic record of any one having been bitten with fatal results.

---

* The Eastern shrikes do not, like the European varieties, store their prey by impaling it on thorns. This may be due to the plentiful supply of food.

† *L. Superciliosus* is the adult of *L. Cristatus.*

Non-Venomous Snakes.

Mame.	Average Length.	
The Python *(Python reticulatus)**	12 to 14 feet.	Not common.
Curtus' Python (*Python curtus*)	6 „	Rare.
Swamp Snake (*Dipsas dendrophila*)	6 „	Common.
Rat Snake (*Ptyas korros*) ...	7 „	Not common.
Green Grass Snake (*Tragops prasinus*)	7 to 9 „	Common.
Painted Tree Snake (*Dendrophis picta*)	3 „	Not uncommon.
Bronzed Tree Snake (*D. caudolineata*)	4 to 5 „	Rare.
Spotted Tree Snake (*Chrysoplœa ornata*)	3 „	Not uncommon.
Variable Ground Snake (*Lycodon aulicus*)†	3 to 4 „	Very rare.
Pond Snake (*Tropidonotus quincunciatus*)‡	3 „	Not common.

Venomous Snakes.

The Black Cobra (*Naja sputatrix*)§	4 to 5 feet.	Common.
The Hamadryad (*Ophiophagus elaps*)‖	9 to 10 „	Rare.
Banded Bungarus (*B. fasciatus*)	3 to 4 „	Rare.
Red-headed Callophis (*C. bivirgatus*)	3 „	Not uncommon.
Brown-headed Callophis (*C. intestinalis*)	2 „	Rare.
Slender Callophis (*C. gracilis*)	2½ „	Very rare.

* Often, but erroneously, called the Boa-constrictor. The Malay name is *Ular Sawah*. A specimen 22 feet long is in the Museum.

† This snake and the preceding are very variable species; 6 well-defined varieties of the former and 7 of the latter are known.

‡ To this list should be added the *Simotes octolineatus*, a specimen of which the writer killed near the Gardens.

§ Malay name *Ular sendok—i.e.*, spoon snake.

‖ The most deadly of the Singapore snakes. It is very fierce and aggressive. Specimens over 14 feet in length have been obtained.

Banded Pit Viper (*Trimeresurus wagleri*)	3 feet.	Fairly common.
Green Pit Viper (*T. Gramineus*)	$2\frac{1}{2}$ "	Rather rare.
Purple Pit Viper (*T. Purpureus*)	$2\frac{1}{2}$ "	Rare.

Hydrophidœ (Sea Snakes).

Banded Sea Snake (*Hydrophis stokesii*)	5 feet.	Very common.

Many other snakes occur in the seas round Singapore, but they are less common than *Stokesii*. They are all venomous.

The common Indian Toad (*Bufo melanostictus*) is abundant. Of Frogs, a considerable number both of terrestrial and arboreal species occur; but the only ones calling for special attention are *Rana pulchra** (a species said to have been introduced from Malacca, and which has multiplied to such an extent as to become a plague) and *R. laticeps* a very large species, measuring, in length of body over 6 in. and across the head nearly 4 in. The hind legs are 9 in. long.

The Crocodile† (*Crocodilus porosus*) is common in the creeks and mangrove swamps. Many other lizards occur; among which may be noted the large water-lizard‡ (*Hydrosaurus salvator*) attaining a length of 6 or 7 feet, the green lizard (*Bronchocela cristatella*), the two flying lizards, *Dracovolans* and *D. blanfordi*. Skinks (*Scincidœ*) are very numerous. Geckos are also numerous, and several species occur; those inhabiting buildings are of small size, but some found in the forest (as *G. stentor* and *G. guttatus*) attain a considerable size. The edible turtle (*Chelonia virgata*) is abundant; the great leathery turtle (*Dermatochelys coriacea*) has been obtained: the hawk's bill turtle (*Caretta squamata*), which yields the best tortoise-shell, is also found. River turtle and land tortoises occur, but do not appear to be numerous

INSECTS.—Insects of all kinds abound in Singapore. About 200 species of Butterflies occur, the most conspicuous being the Ornithopteras. The Moths are more numerous still.

---

* Popularly called the bull-frog in Singapore. Its booming is heard all over the island after rain.

† Commonly, but erroneously, called the Alligator.

‡ Usually called the Iguana or, more properly, the Monitor.

Four species of true silk worm moths occur; the most common is the large *Attacus atlas*, the expanse of the wing in the female being 9½ inches or more. Wasps and hornets are very numerous; one of the most common and conspicuous being *Vespa cincta*, which builds a huge nest of mud, the walls being very thin, but bearing without injury the violence of tropical showers. Flies are abundant, and some, like *Stilbum splendidum*, very beautiful. Beetles are numerous, and some species, like *Rhyncophorus* and *Xylotrupes*, do great damage by attacking the coconut palms. There are three species of honey-bees, and four of carpenter-bees* (*Xylocarpa*). Ants are numerous in varieties and individuals. The caringa or red ant gives a painful sting when touched. Termites† (so called white ants) abound everywhere, and do a great deal of damage to property.

Spiders abound everywhere in Singapore, the most conspicuous being the large garden spiders. A huge black nocturnal spider also occurs. Centipedes are not uncommon though they seldom invade dwellings; the large black and red *Scolopendræ* sometimes attain 9 in in length. The large black scorpion is fairly common, and several smaller species occur, one of which, a small pale green one, is not unfrequently found in houses, in damp places, such as bath-rooms, &c.

FISH.—The seas around Singapore contain a great variety of fish of many wonderful forms and colours. Large quantities are daily brought into the markets.

Several species of sharks occur; the spotted shark (*Stegostoma tigrina*) and two others, *Carcharias acutidens* and *C. macloti*, are perhaps the most common. The hammerheaded shark (*Zygæna malleus*) is also found. Two, and probably three, species of sword-fish occur—*Histiophorus gladius*‡ and *H. immaculatus*. Two species of saw-fish§ are found, *Pristis perotteti* and *P. zysron*. The garfish||

---

* These do considerable damage by boring into the woodwork of houses.

† It is hardly necessary to mention that the Termites are not ants proper; they belong to the order Neuroptera, while the ants belong to the order Hymenoptera.

‡ The *Ikan todak* of Malay legend.

§ The saws of these fish are usually brought for sale by natives to the steamers in port.

|| The force with which the garfish propel themselves out of the water is very great. It is said that men have been killed in open boats by a blow from garfish skipping over the sea.

found in these waters are of two forms—*Belone* (5 species at least) and *Hemiramphus* (8 species). In the skates there is a great diversity of form and size. Some of the species, from the spines with which the tail is armed, are able to inflict painful and serious wounds. The ox-skate or sea devil (*Dicerobatis eregoodoo*) is 20 feet in expanse. The commonest of the skates in the Singapore seas are *Rhynocobatus anchylostomus* and *Rhinobatus thounii*. The Baracoota (*Sphyræna commersoni*) deserves special mention here. The jaws of this fish are armed with a double row of teeth with sharp cutting edges. The natives greatly dread it, as it attacks people without hesitation, inflicting serious wounds. Its length is about 4 feet. Of prawns and crayfish several species occur, the crayfish growing to a very large size (often to more than a foot in length). Both shore and sea crabs are abundant in numbers and in varieties.

II.—THE FLORA OF SINGAPORE ISLAND.

(*By* H. N. RIDLEY, ESQ., F.L.S., *Director of Gardens.*)

One of the first things that strikes a visitor is the richness and variety of the tints of the foliage. Each tree seems to be different from the one next to it; and indeed, the number of different kinds is very large in comparison with that of a more temperate region.

As there are no seasons here, the heat and dampness of the climate causes continual growth, so that the greater part of the flora consists of evergreen trees and shrubs. Some few trees shed all their leaves at one time, and after remaining leafless for one or two days, are speedily clothed again with young leaves—often of brilliant red or pink tints—which very soon assume their green colour. The larger number of trees, however, shed and renew their leaves continuously throughout the year, and are therefore evergreens.

The apparent scantiness of flowers here has often been noticed. This is due to several causes—one of which is that the greater proportion of the flowers are small, and concealed in the wealth of foliage; and even when they are large and abundant they are often placed so high upon the trees that they are invisible from below. Many plants, again, though producing during the year large quantities of blossoms, bear so few at a time that they are never conspicuous. Lastly, owing to heat and moisture the flowers are very short lived—many lasting only for a few hours in the early morning.

At one time the whole island of Singapore was densely wooded, but, through cultivation, much of the primæval jungle has been destroyed. The best accessible example of primitive forest is to be found on the hill, Bukit Timah, seven miles from town:

Here may be seen many lofty trees of the order *Dipterocarpeæ*, with straight smooth stems rising unbranched for ninety feet or more. They supply the valuable timbers known as Serayah and Meranti, and also exude a resin known as Dammar which is exported from Singapore for making varnish. Most kinds flower once in five or six years, the flowers are often large and sweet-scented, and are followed by the curious red two-winged fruit, from which the order takes its name. Another remarkable tree of the same shape is the Cumpas (*Cumpassia malaccensis*), the wood of which is too hard to cut, so that it may often be seen standing alone in cultivated land having escaped through its hardness the axe of the planter. Sometimes one may pick up in the woods the large fruit of the Woody Durian-tree (*Neesia*), a bluish grey, smooth or warty pod, which splits half way down into four or five lobes, disclosing a number of small red seeds surrounded by irritating yellow hairs. Oaks, chestnuts, figs, tree-myrtles (*Eugenia*), ebonies, and innumerable other trees go to make up the tree-flora of these jungles. Of the smaller shrubs, very showy are the orange flowered *Ixoras; Randia macrophylla*, with great white trumpets spotted inside with black; *Ardisias*, with pink flowers and scarlet berries (called by the natives "Mouse-deer's eyes"); *Wormia*, a big shrub with large yellow flowers, and very many less conspicuous plants.

Innumerable climbing plants ascend to the top of the trees, and most important among them are the climbing palms known as rattans (*Calamus*). The biggest is *Plectocomia*, with a strong stem about four inches in diameter, covered with sharp spines, It may be seen towering far above the forest. The flowers are arranged in long brown hanging tails about 10 feet in length, and when the fruit is ripe the whole plant dies. Other climbers are the strychnine plant (*Strychnos Tieute*), with deep green leaves, and curious round ball-like fruit of a greyish green colour. *Gambirs*, *Bauhinias*, Menispermacious plants, one of which, *Fibraurea*, produces from its stem a good yellow dye, a *Stephanotis*, many climbing apocynaceous plants, with white or rosy flowers, often scented, among which are the *Willughbeias*, from which is obtained the gutta-grip, a valuable kind of India-rubber, jasmines, wax plants (*Hoya*) and many others. The pitcher plants (*Nepenthes*) of which there are five kinds in Singapore are also climbers. All are common and generally to be found in damp open places. It may be as well to remind visitors that the cups are portions of the leaves modified beautifully as insect traps, and are not the flowers, which are small purple or green blooms arranged in thick spikes.

In damp and rocky spots a great many curious and beautiful herbaceous plants can be found—gingers (*Amomum*), with tall leafy stems and tufts of scarlet, pink or white flowers almost hidden in the ground; *Globbas*, with nodding spikes of white or orange flowers in shape like some strange insect; *Aroids*, with heart-shaped, or arrow-shaped leaves, small ground-orchids, of which the *Anœctochili*, with their ovate, deep purple leaves, veined with gold; and *Plocoglottis*, with large lanceolate leaves looking when seen against the sunlight like patches of purple stained-glass, are the most attractive.

FERNS are very plentiful in Singapore and range from tall tree ferns (*Alsophila*), *Angiopteris*, the Elephant fern, with its short round stem and huge twelve foot-fronds, and the great birds' nest fern (*Thamnopteris nidus-avis*) to tiny polypodies and filmy ferns:

Well worthy of notice, are the elks' horns (*Platycerium*), the water fern (*Ceratopteris*) growing in the ditches, the climbing *Lygodiums*, *Dipteris Horsfieldii* growing in masses on rocky banks near the sea; the bracken-like *Gleichenias* and the elegant *Davallias.* Selaginellas too are very abundant and varied; and there are several kinds of Club-moss (*Lycopodium*), some of which hang from the trees; but the commonest is *L. cernuum*, growing abundantly in the open grassy spots, and often collected for house decoration.

ORCHIDS are abundant in Singapore, but chiefly grow in the mangrove swamps. Many have inconspicuous flowers, but there are some of the orchid lovers' greatest favourites:

The commonest is the well-known Pigeon orchid (*Dendrobum crumenatum*), clothing the trees even in the town of Singapore. *D. Dalhousieanum*, with its great cream and maroon flowers, finest of all Dendrobes, has been met with in the jungles, but is very rare. Erias with spikes of small white flowers; the Leopard orchid, *Grammatophyllum*, biggest of all orchids, with its great racemes, eight feet high, of yellow and brown flowers; *Saccolabium giganteum*, with thick spikes of pink-spotted white blossoms; curious *Cirrhopetala*, with strangely moving lips; *Cymbidium aloifolium*, with long narrow leaves and pendulous racemes of brown and purple flowers, are among the finest of the tree orchids. Of ground-orchids, none are more likely to attract attention than the beautiful pink *Spathoglottis plicata* and *Bromheadia palustris*, with large white, yellow and violet flowers, both of which grow in grassy open places, and are constantly in flower, while the lovely apricot-coloured *Calanthe curculigoides* may reward the orchid hunter who dives into the dense wet thickets in November.

Besides orchids many other plants grow upon the trees, being epiphytic:

Very rare is the splendid crimson *Rhododendron*, high up out of reach on the highest trees. The ants' nest plant, *Hydnophytum*, is a curious epiphyte, the base of the stem is swollen into a fleshy mass often as big as a man's head, which when cut open is seen to be a real vegetable ant's nest swarming with minute, but ferocious ants. *Dischidia Rafflesiana*, the bladder plant, is remarkable for its leaves modified into strange yellow conical bladders.

There are many kinds of Palms, of which may be specially mentioned the sealing-wax palm (*Cyrtostachys*) with its bright red stems; the Corintin (*Drymophlœus Singaporianus*), with feathery leaves and slender black stems from which elegant walking sticks can be made; the thorny-stemmed Nibong (*Oncosperma tigillaria*), much used for house building, and the Penang Lawyers (*Licuala*). Another useful group of plants is that of the Screw pines or Pandans, of which four or five kinds inhabit damp spots, the biggest is the Mengkuang (*Pandanus furcatus*), the long narrow leaves of which are much used for making *Kajangs*,* baskets, hats and innumerable other things.

The number of grasses and sedges is rather small, as these are not plentiful in jungle-country, but one kind is too conspicuous by its presence. The Lalang grass (*Imperata cylindrica*) covers great tracts of country, rapidly springing up wherever the forest has been cleared. It is almost useless for any purpose and, when it has taken hold of the ground, is with difficulty eradicated.

A large portion of the shores of the island are covered with Mangrove swamps; and the peculiarities of this class of vegetation can well be studied here. The trees which compose it though having at first sight a great similarity belong to several different groups. The true Mangrove trees, *Rhizophora* and *Bruguiera*, are remarkable for the seed germinating while still on the tree, and sending

* The *Kajang* is "a most useful contrivance.........used for boat or cart coverings. It folds up, and in the jungle answers the purpose of a tent."—*Swettenham.*

down a long green cigar-shaped root. Mangrove-wood is much used for firewood, and the bark supplies tanning material. In these swamps grow, also, the Nireh-tree (*Carapa*), conspicuous from its large brown cannon-ball like fruits. The bark of this tree is a valuable medicine for dysentery.

Many and varied are the cultivated plants to be seen in the gardens in Singapore, and among the most striking are the scarlet-flowered Flame of the Forest (*Poinciana*), the Allamandas from Brazil with their large yellow blossoms, and the quaint Ravenala from Madagascar, the Traveller's-tree, often erroneously taken for a palm. It is really an ally of the Banana, as the shape and texture of its leaves show at once; it has the appearance of a gigantic fan, and derives its English name from the fact that by piercing the base of the leaf-stalk a supply of water can be often obtained. The beverage, however, is hardly to be recommended.

Of the numerous fruits of this region, two especially are famous, the Durian and the Mangosteen. It is worth a voyage to the East, says Wallace, to eat the Durian, and it is certain that it is not worth eating anywhere else. In appearance it suggests a large oval light brown horse chestnut. The tough rind covered with thorns, splits into several lobes, when ripe, and discloses a variable number of large oblong seeds enclosed in a creamy pulp, which is the eatable portion. Many persons are deterred from trying the flavour on account of the disagreeable odour of the rind, but no sooner is the mouth filled with the deliciously flavoured pulp than all sense of the smell disappears. Wallace, in his well-known work on the Malay Archipelago, has endeavoured to describe the flavour of this fruit, but indeed it cannot be described, it must be tasted to be appreciated. By a judge of fruit the Durian will be allowed to take a position in the front rank as one of the first-class fruits of the world.

The Mangosteen is, however, more generally popular with Europeans, and is certainly a most beautiful and refreshing fruit. It is about the size of a moderate-sized apple, round, with a flat top on which is the star-shaped stigma. In colour it is of a deep maroon or black crimson, and when broken across is seen to consist of a variable number of pulpy white pips, each enclosing a seed, arranged in a circle and enveloped in the thick pink rind. The pulp is very sweet and delicately flavoured, the flavour being much improved by putting the fruit in ice for a few hours before eating.

Both the Durian and Mangosteen have distinct though somewhat irregular fruiting periods and as their seasons differ in different parts of the Peninsula, it happens often that the fruits can be obtained almost all through the year.

These notes on the flora serve but to give an indication of the wealth and variety of the vegetation. Few regions contain so large a proportion of interesting plants as that of the Malayan Peninsula; and the study of botany here will well repay its votary.

III.—GEOLOGICAL FEATURES.

The Geology of Singapore is very disappointing to the student. The island consists of a core of grey granite cropping out in the bigger hills, as at Bukit Timah, but the greater portion is covered with stiff yellow and red clays, sands, gravels, and iron stone commonly, but erroneously, called laterite. This formation is evidently derived from destruction of loftier granitic hills, and extends, also, over a large portion of the Peninsula. It is almost entirely destitute of fossils (a few plant remains alone having been met with), and it is impossible at present to conjecture its age.

CHAPTER XV.

Climate, Monsoons, &c.

SINGAPORE is unusually favoured in the matter of climate. Situated close to the Equator, it nevertheless enjoys climatic advantages not shared by other places in the same latitude. The abundant rainfall (the average is over 90 inches annually) tempers the fierce heat of the Tropics; and violent storms are unknown. There is no change of seasons; the island boasts an eternal summer, and is clothed with a perennial green. The thermometer (in the shade) ranges between 80° and 90° (Fahr.) during the day, and between 70° and 80° at night: it has never been known to rise above 94° or to fall below 63°. The mornings are generally fresh and cool; and after sunset light breezes come from the sea to cool the air. The sheltered position of Singapore secures for it these advantages, and others alluded to in Chapter I.

Though there is no marked change of seasons, yet the influence of the monsoons, or trade winds, is felt in Singapore. The change of the monsoon is accompanied by heavy and prolonged rains; but since rain falls all the year round, a slight increase in the fall at particular periods is hardly noticeable. The North-east Monsoon blows from November to April, during which time the Singapore winds usually sit in that quarter; but by no means invariably. The South-west Monsoon blows from

May to October, and with it come the winds known locally as Sumatras and Java winds. The Sumatra is a rapid squall from the south or south-west, accompanied by heavy rain and generally thunder. It sweeps swiftly across the Strait and the island, and rarely lasts more than an hour or two. On reaching the land, it hardly lasts so long. The Sumatras spring up towards evening, or during the night; they are the most violent winds that visit Singapore; but they are mild compared with the gales that periodically sweep over the British Isles from the Atlantic. Occasionally very heavy rain-storms visit Singapore On the 29th of May, 1892, in the short space of six hours, the rain-gauges registered a fall of nearly nine inches. A great part of the town and island was flooded; in some of the public thoroughfares the depth of water for some hours ranged from 18 inches to 4 feet.

The Java winds blow from the south or south-east from May to September. They are generally supposed to be unhealthy; but though fever is commoner from May to September than during the rest of the year, it is not certain that this is due to the prevalence of these winds. The effect of the Java wind is first a pleasant sensation of coolness, and then a hot, disagreeable feeling of "stickiness" all over the body. Passing from a shady place to the open, where the Java wind blows, people feel sometimes as if they were approaching the blast of a furnace; the air is stifling. It may be doubted whether the ill-effects of these winds go further than the unpleasant sensation above described.

The day is practically of uniform length throughout the year—twelve hours of daylight. The sun rises about 6 a.m., and sets about 6 p.m.; with a few minutes' variation during the year as it passes from the tropic of Cancer to the tropic of Capricorn and back. Darkness falls rapidly after the sun disappears below the horizon, with almost no intermediate twilight. The heat is greatest during the early afternoon; but by 4.30 p.m., the sun is far down and the air cool enough to admit of out-door recreation. The early morning, until an hour after sun rise (*i.e.* till 7 a.m.) is fresh and cool, and is the best time of day for walking, riding or shooting. The heavy dew that falls during the night, however, prevents out-door sports such as tennis or cricket in the morning.

Singapore should be one of the healthiest places in tropical latitudes and is so for Europeans. Cholera, the scourge of the East, is almost unknown, owing to the abundant rainfall; and dysentery is rare. The annual death rate is estimated at 47 per thousand. The growth of the town, slackness in instituting adequate sanitary measures, and the presence of dust make this greater than it should be. The chief disadvantage of the climate to Europeans and others accustomed to change of seasons is the absence of any such change in Singapore; the effect of the eternal summer is somewhat relaxing and enervating to those who have come from temperate regions.

CHAPTER XVI.

THE MALAY LANGUAGE AND LITERATURE.

THE Malay Language, often called the Italian of the East, on account of its broad vowels and soft consonants, is, in its many dialects, one of the most widely spoken Asiatic tongues. Throughout the Malay Peninsula and Archipelago, in parts of Siam, and even in such remote places as Formosa, Madagascar and Cape Colony, varieties of the language are to be found. Its origin is obscure, and will probably remain so, until the origin of the Malay people is discovered. The Malays themselves consider Sumatra as the cradle of their race; but this means no more than that they found themselves in Sumatra when the self-consciousness of the race emerged from the infancy of barbarism. Philologists have difficulty in classifying the language. Attempts have been made to affiliate it to the monosyllabic languages of China, Annam, and Siam; and no doubt there is a considerable Mongolian element in Malay, though there is a large admixture of other elements. The use of numeral co-efficients to express the plural is unquestionably Mongolian in origin. For example, the Malays say—*Perampuan tiga orang* (woman three person) for three women; *kuda lima ekor* (horse five tail) for five horses; *Telor sa' puloh biji* (egg ten seed) for ten eggs; *cf.*, the concession to Chinese idiom in Pidgin English "Three piecee man" for three men. The question whether all languages were not originally monosyllabic is one that divides philologists, but at any rate Malay, notwithstanding the Mongolian element, is now dissyllabic; and in regard to accent, trochaic. This, in connection with its broad vowels and soft consonants, is the secret of its musical sound.

Not only is the ear charmed by the music and rhythm of the spoken tongue, but the mind is also delighted by the simple and graceful forms of speech, expressing highly poetical ideas, which are often on the lips of a people not conspicuously romantic or imaginative. Many of the common words and phrases of ordinary life are, from a western point of view, highly poetical, owing to the child-like, but artistic combination of ideas that are not naturally connected. The Malay, for example, calls the sun *Mata-hari*. "the eye of day:" he speaks of a brook as *anak sungei*, "the son of a river;" when he is sorrowful or angry he says he is *susah hati or sakit hati*, "sick at heart." An eclipse of the sun or moon he regards as a temporary illness of these bodies—*sakit mata-hari*, *sakit bulan*. Such idiomatic and poetical expressions form one of the chief characteristics of the language.

Malay, as spoken in the Straits Settlements, in the Peninsula, and in many of the islands in the Archipelago, has been greatly modified, and its vocabulary has been largely enriched by the influence of foreign languages. The Hindu conquest of Malaya, many centuries ago, imported Sanskrit words and ideas into the language. (The introduction to W. E. Maxwell's "Manual of the Malay Language" gives a careful and scholarly account of the nature and extent of Sanscrit influence.) In the thirteenth century came the Mahommedan supremacy, during which the most of the Malays embraced Islam;

and consequently borrowed largely from the Arabic language to supply deficiencies in their own. Later still, European influence made itself apparent,—Portuguese, Dutch and English words being freely adopted to express ideas introduced by the foreigners. In Singapore the Malay colloquial is a hybrid language: few of the great languages of the world are unrepresented in its vocabulary. The purest Malay is spoken in Perak, the most northern of the Native States under British Protection.

Malay is free from inflections, and, like most primitive languages, poor in connectives. The juxtaposition of two words is generally enough to imply their connection. The verb is simple compared with the elaborate conjugations of the perfect classical languages of the East and West, Arabic and Greek; it is not declined at all; its tenses are expressed by means of auxiliaries, and its modes by prefixes. Number is indicated by numerals, with or without numeral co-efficients; sometimes (indefinitely) by re-duplication: gender. by the addition of the word "male" or "female," and that only when distinction of sex is required by the context; and case is not indicated at all, except, perhaps, by the position of the word in the sentence.* The best Malay Grammar and Dictionary (by the late Dr. Marsden †) are now

* Malay has been called "a most ungrammatical but most idiomatic language." This is true if inflections only constitute grammar. An ungrammatical language is one without laws either of syntax or of idiom; and that Malay certainly is not.

† Dr. Marsden was a contemporary of Sir Stamford Raffles; his Grammar and Dictionary were published in 1812, and deal with the language as he knew it in Sumatra. The Peninsular Malay differs considerably from the Sumatran; but Marsden's works might be re-printed with such additions as are necessary for students of the language as it is now spoken and written in Malaya.

out of print. Copies may be bought occasionally, but at a prohibitive price. Mr. W. E. Maxwell, a former Colonial Secretary of the Straits Settlements; Sir F. A. Swettenham, Resident-General F. M. S., and Governor, S. S.; Mr. R. J. Wilkinson, formerly Inspector of Schools; and Mr. W. G. Shellabear, of the Methodist Episcopal Mission, have all published works which give a fair introduction to the spoken language; but there is still room for a historical and scientific grammar, and for a larger dictionary, Visitors to the Straits Settlements will find the small hand-book published by Messrs. Fraser and Neave, Ltd., Singapore, a useful guide to the colloquial.

The literature of the Malays is extensive and copious, but not rich. It consists of heroic tales and legends, works on ethics and laws, and a large number of proverbs and poems. Of the literature as a whole it may be said that it is imitative rather than original; and this may be accounted for by the fact that the Malays have not for many centuries enjoyed an independent national existence; and, also perhaps, by the fact that the art of writing was unknown to them till they came into contact with nations more powerful and more civilised than themselves; and contact of that kind means conquest. It is probable that the acquisition of the art of writing dates from the Mahommedan invasion in the thirteenth century.* Malay is written in the Arabic character, with a few modifications of some letters to represent sounds not found in the latter tongue. The vowel points are not in general use; consequently there

* This is disputed by some who claim to have found traces of an earlier Malay writing.

is considerable uncertainty as to the correct orthography.

The chronicles and legends are said to be painfully genealogical and as tedious and uninteresting to the Western reader as a Chinese drama to a European spectator. They have, however, an interest of their own, and are not without literary grace. The best known to Europeans is the *Hikayat** of Abdullah bin Abdul Kader, written in the year 1840. The author was the *Munshi* who taught Malay to the earliest British settlers in Singapore. This is not his only work, but, owing to its being used as a reading-book in the Colony, it is better known than the others. Another chronicle worthy of mention is the *Sejarat Malayu* (Malay Annals), a mixture of history and legend.†

Besides the chronicles, legends, and other prose writings, there is a large number of proverbs, poems (*shäer*)‡ and *pantuns*. The last-named, the *pantuns*, consist of a verse, or verses, of four lines each, rhyming alternately, and couched in highly metaphorical language, to discover the meaning of which often baffles the Western reader. Three specimens follow §:—

The heron flies into the air,
  And dashes down the fish it had caught.
Forbear to grasp burning embers,
  Or, feeling the heat, you will quickly let them go.

---

* The word *Hikayat*, used by the Malays, is the Arabic word for story. A translation of the greater part of Abdullah's *Hikayat*, by J. T. Thomson, F.R.G.S., is published by Henry S. King & Co.

† See notes on p. 7 and p. 66.

‡ *Shäer* is also from the Arabic.

§ Taken from the Appendix to Marsden's Malay Grammar.

A maiden draws water from the well;
The bucket falls off, leaving only the cord.
Consent, my life, to the departure of your friend,
And do not grieve at the separation.

A white horse whose hoofs are black
Is a horse for the Sultan Iskander.
My love is dark; various are her blandishments;
But she is incapable of speaking the truth.

A valuable collection of Malay manuscripts, made by Sir Stamford Raffles, was lost to the world by a most regrettable accident. The East Indiaman on which Raffles had embarked for England with his collection, took fire at sea; and though he escaped with the rest of the passengers and the crew, the manuscripts were destroyed.

The Malays may often be heard reading far into the night. One man reads aloud to a company of listeners; and the method of reading is a kind of chanting or intoning.

Sir Frank Swettenham's "British Malaya" (1907); Mr. W. W. Skeat's "Malay Magic" and "Fairy Tales;" Skeat and Blagden's "Pagan Races of the Malay Peninsula;" Wilkinson's "Malay Literature" and "Malay Beliefs" are the chief recent works on the Malay.

ADVERTISEMENTS.